LADY JANE GREY

Hester Chapman is the author of several historical works including a study of Edward VI which won the 1958 W. H.
Heinemann Foundation prize, a widely acclaimed biography
of Henry VIII and this biography of Lady Jane Grey, which
was a Book Society choice. Her novel, *Eugénie*, based on the
life of Napoleon III's wife, was a bestseller.

Born in Dorset and educated privately, Hester Chapman has
had a variety of jobs – secretary, telephone operator, waitress,
mannequin in Paris, governess, and schoolmistress. She loves
travelling, and when not writing spends much of her time
collecting china and paintings. She lives in London.

'Hester Chapman's integrity as a biographer is well known;
she is steeped in the Tudor period and has the art of making it
immediate and comprehensible . . . the whole theme of the book
is an arresting one.' – *Daily Telegraph*

'Shrewd and beautifully written' – *Sunday Express*

'Excellent . . . gives a very clear analysis of Tudor power politics' – *Punch*

'A brilliant picture of the household of a great English nobleman in the first flush of the Reformation' – *New Statesman*

'The first real picture of Queen Jane to have been
presented with the backing of scholarship, as competent foot-
notes, bibliography and index will testify' – *The Times
Educational Supplement*

CONDITIONS OF SALE

LADY JANE GREY

October 1537 - February 1554

HESTER W. CHAPMAN

UNABRIDGED

PAN BOOKS LTD : LONDON

First published 1962 by Jonathan Cape Ltd.
This edition published 1972 by Pan Books Ltd,
33 Tothill Street, London, SW1.

ISBN 0 330 02987 8

For help and advice, special thanks are due to Miss
Helen Lehmann and Mr George Rylands.

Printed and bound in England by
Hazell Watson and Viney Ltd,
Aylesbury, Bucks

TO INEZ JENKINS

Be absolute for death; either death or life
Shall thereby be the sweeter. Reason thus with life:
If I do lose thee, I do lose a thing
That none but fools would keep . . .

Measure for Measure, III.i

Contents

LIST OF ILLUSTRATIONS
(between pages 98 and 99)

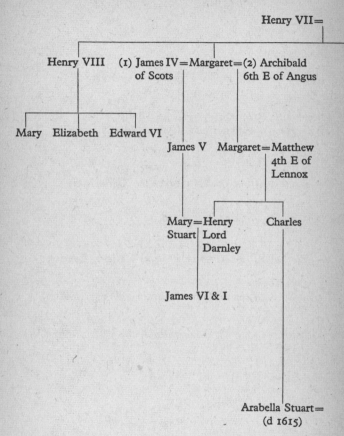

Henry VII=

Henry VIII   (1) James IV=Margaret=(2) Archibald
             of Scots   6th E of Angus

Mary   Elizabeth   Edward VI

James V   Margaret=Matthew
                        4th E of
                        Lennox

Mary=Henry   Charles
Stuart   Lord
       Darnley

James VI & I

Arabella Stuart=
(d 1615)

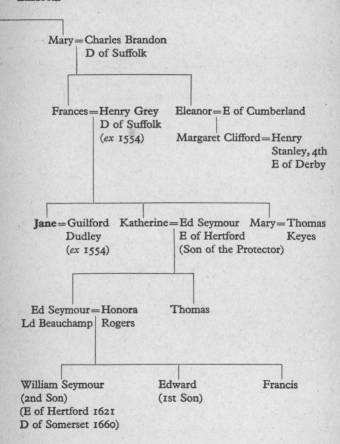

Elizabeth

Mary=Charles Brandon
D of Suffolk

Frances=Henry Grey   Eleanor=E of Cumberland
D of Suffolk
(*ex* 1554)   Margaret Clifford=Henry
Stanley, 4th
E of Derby

Jane=Guilford   Katherine=Ed Seymour   Mary=Thomas
Dudley   E of Hertford   Keyes
(*ex* 1554)   (Son of the Protector)

Ed Seymour=Honora   Thomas
Ld Beauchamp Rogers

William Seymour   Edward   Francis
(2nd Son)   (1st Son)
(E of Hertford 1621
D of Somerset 1660)

Foreword

LADY JANE GREY, eldest daughter of the Duke and Duchess of Suffolk and great-niece of Henry VIII, was born in 1537 and executed at the age of sixteen and a half. She has been the subject of a play, two operas and a number of poems and memoirs. At one time her correspondence was constantly reprinted and fragments of her conversation were quoted again and again. Now her nine days' reign, recorded in detail by contemporary historians, is treated as an unimportant interlude between the death of Edward VI and the accession of Mary I. Seldom criticized, always pitied and never censured, she has become the prototype of the persecuted heroine, the supreme example of a political pawn, an intellectual phenomenon and a blameless martyr.

She was all these: but she was something more. For four hundred years there has been an instinctive withdrawal from certain aspects of her character; the floods of compassionate praise poured over her by historians and biographers have obscured both her personality and her spiritual worth; and her admirers seem to have ignored the strange exuberance, the steely determination which enabled her to disregard, to withstand and at last to dominate those in authority over her. Bullied, flattered, used, traduced and butchered, this child and victim of the English Reformation moved alone through its triumphs and horrors, as detached in her self-judgement as in her condemnation of those who exploited and destroyed her. It therefore follows that the qualities which helped to produce her superb dignity and her almost inhuman resolution were not all attractive, or even desirable. So the conditions in which these qualities were formed must be seen as they appeared to the persons responsible for them, because their hopes and schemes are the mainspring of her story. Her tragedy was symbolic: for she was not merely an innocent and pitiable figure; she was, as she herself declared, a conscious and at one point an active participator in the revolutions which brought her to the block. It is in the light of that awareness, and of her acceptance of her Tudor heritage, that she must finally be judged.

Part I

The Years of Preparation

> Thus saith the Lord to His anointed ... I will go before thee, and make the crooked places straight ... And I will give thee the treasures of darkness, and hidden riches of secret places.
>
> *Isaiah* xlv. 1–3

Chapter 1

The Greys, the Brandons and the Tudors

I N the sixteenth century the Tower of London was one of the prettiest sights in England. Set between neat gabled houses and lawns sloping down to the crowded glitter of the Thames, its moat, its outer walls, it triangular courtyards and flagged cupolas created a design in which elegance and strength were perfectly combined. More graceful than most fortresses, less grandiose than the neighbouring palaces, it dominated a richly coloured panorama extending from the cold splendour of Westminster to the romantic elaborations of Greenwich. The Tower was the focal point of an infinitely variegated city planned round the river and encircled by fields, forests, marshes and hills.

A general view showed nothing ramshackle or sprawling in this display, of which the effect was achieved by a series of architectural climaxes. At intervals the rows of squat, timbered houses were overshadowed by taller, slenderer buildings of brick and Portland stone; these generally surrounded or led up to a church, a prison or a hospital which sheltered, a little severely, the structures beneath them. Each tower and spire and buttress sprang from a cluster of humbler dwellings, subordinated yet looking upwards. The artisan's booth was protected by the merchant's workrooms, which depended on the nobleman's mansion, while this in turn emulated the soaring wonders of the royal residences. The palaces of the patricians were newer than those of the monarchy and enormously varied; towering, battlemented strongholds, of which the inspiration seemed rather Norman French than Tudor English, alternated with the informal, comfortable modernity of homes designed for entertainment and ease; these converted convents and monasteries contrasted with and set off the stateliness of the earlier pleasure-domes, perhaps because they were embowered in trees, flower-beds and pleached alleys leading down to the clear water through gates of marble or rusticated stone. Their colouring ranged from pure white to deep cream and pearl grey, and they embodied all the contemporary ideals of luxury and ostentation, in spite of the fact that many of them were surrounded by crumbling wooden hovels of horrible squalor. But their river façades were beautiful; and the back courtyards made an adequate barrier between their owners' quiet and the prowling incursions of their criminal or starving neighbours. Elsewhere, privacy and segregation were unknown. The nobleman shared streets and waterways with the common rabble. Ragged, filthy and obscene caricatures of humanity jostled gorgeously furred and jewelled courtiers and statesmen, pressed against the velvet trappings of their horses and gaped at their brilliantly sweeping ladies, without resentment and without much subservience. And all, passing under Tower Bridge or Temple Bar, were reminded, if they chose to look upwards, of fate's revenges and of the imminence of mortality by the grinning, putrescent heads – some of them years old and semi-skeletal – of those who had imperilled the safety of the realm or incurred the sovereign's displeasure.

Finally, as if to epitomize the picture of a community in which all had an allotted place, London Bridge, that miracle of engineering, with St Mary Overy on one side of the river and St Magnus on the other, contained every kind of accommodation and was a city within a city, of tenements, guardhouses, churches, shops, markets and wharves. The majority of its inhabitants neither knew nor desired existence elsewhere; many of them never in their lives set foot beyond its confines.

London Bridge was the penultimate stage in the city's progress, the preliminary to the Tower, which at first glance seemed to provide an agreeable and dignified conclusion – until suddenly, a gaping archway, black, dripping, dreadful, met the eye: Traitors' Gate, a portent of doom, disgrace and – what our sixteenth-century ancestors feared more than either of these – failure in the ceaseless struggle for wealth and power.

Seven months before her death Lady Jane Grey passed by

this gate, entering the Tower over the drawbridge; its jaws then closed upon her. She had reached it by a route which ended in the city, stopping at a number of palaces: Durham House, Baynard's Castle, Westminster, Sion, Suffolk Place. That journey began fifteen years earlier, a hundred miles away, at the manor of Bradgate in Leicestershire.

ii

In 1530 – twenty-one years before he became Duke of Suffolk – the father of Lady Jane, Henry Grey, third Marquess of Dorset, took possession of Bradgate. The late Marquess, Thomas Grey, had built but not quite completed a mansion which combined the amenities of a hunting-palace with the comforts of a private villa. It housed some three hundred servants and its outer structure included a tiltyard, an enormous gatehouse and two ornamental towers. The birthplace of Lady Jane and her sisters overlooked six miles of park, the slate quarries owned by the family and a lake, beyond which lay the forest of Chartley. Between that richly stocked wilderness and the park was a huddle of cottages; the house itself was surrounded by gardens laid out in the formal, modern style and bordered by a brook. Ferns, rocks and ancient oaks made a pleasant background for the rose-coloured brick walls and white stone facings of the new lord's inheritance, which he began to improve on and elaborate (he did not trouble to repair the cottages) soon after he was established. Bradgate, five miles from the city of Leicester, was remote, but not desolate or bleak. The hunting was of the best and most varied in England; and the prospects, which comprised valleys, streams and woods, were noble and impressive.[1]

A rather uncertain and hazardous existence at Court and in the French wars, alternating with abortive intrigue for further favours, had given Dorset ambition without stability of purpose. Handsome, affable, cultivated, impetuous and far too easy-going, he had competed for wealth and position intermittently and with only moderate success. In these days of the rising 'new men' he counted himself as one of the old nobility: for his grandfather, the first Marquess, was the son of Elizabeth Woodville and therefore the stepson of Edward IV, Henry VIII's maternal grandfather.

Three years after he succeeded, young Dorset, who in addition to his marquisate and his other estates in Leicestershire had inherited the baronies of Ferrers, Grey of Groby, Astley, Boneville and Harrington, dissolved his contract of betrothal with Lady Katherine Fitzalan in order to ally himself with the King's elder niece, Frances Brandon; they were married in the chapel of his London house in Southwark. This lady's ancestry combined royal and middle-class blood – in the current phrase, 'cloth of gold with cloth of frieze' – and, from her husband's point of view, her kinship with the King was of incalculable value; its results were to prove fatal to every member of her family but herself.

Frances Brandon was the elder daughter of Charles Brandon, Duke of Suffolk (a country gentleman ennobled by Henry VIII) and Henry's younger sister, Mary Tudor, formerly Queen of France, whose marriage to Louis XII lasted three months, leaving her free to give her hand to Suffolk as soon as her period of mourning was over. This young man, Lady Jane's maternal grandfather and Henry's closest friend, was an extremely shady character. He had divorced two wives and buried a third before he married the Queen Dowager, by whom he had two daughters, Frances and Eleanor. In 1535 Mary died and Brandon married a fifth wife, Lady Katherine Willoughby d'Eresby, by whom he had two sons. By that time Frances and Henry Dorset had been married two years and she had borne him a son who died a few months later; a daughter followed, who also died. Lady Jane was born in the same year and the same month – the exact date in October 1537 is not recorded – as Edward VI, Henry's son by his third wife, Jane Seymour. Although the Dorsets were disappointed at not having a son, they had important plans for Jane. From their point of view, the dynastic situation was promising, and they were bent on getting the most out of it.

Edward VI, who was to succeed Henry VIII in 1547 at the age of nine, was regarded by many and possibly by Henry himself as his only rightful heir; for his half-sisters, Mary and Elizabeth, had both been declared illegitimate. Some years before Henry died he caused Parliament to pass an Act which enabled him to leave the crown by will and thus, if he saw fit, to cut out his two daughters. In fact, he did not do so. In his will he left the crown to Edward, Mary and Elizabeth, in that order. In the event of none of them having any heirs the succession came to Frances Dorset and her children, and then to her younger sister Eleanor, and hers. So in 1547 Jane was, presumptively, fifth in line for the English throne.*

Her parents brought her up, not only with the rather remote possibility of her becoming Queen Regnant in view, but also with the idea that she might marry her cousin Prince Edward – for although Henry VIII was negotiating a foreign alliance for him within a few months of his birth, none of these schemes materialized. And so, during the last years of Henry's reign, the Dorsets' hopes for Jane rose very high, and her education was conducted accordingly. Intellectually, she was trained as if she had been a boy; but her parents' treatment of her destroyed much of the happiness she might have derived from such a training; for Frances Dorset was a harsh, grasping, brutal woman who dominated her capricious and extravagant husband.

Her portrait gives the impression of being a good likeness, partly because it illustrates her behaviour to her children. As a young woman, the Lady Frances resembled her floridly handsome father; her physical vitality and her tireless enjoyment of open-air sports and indoor games may have engendered a surface gaiety; and she must have had some social charm, for she was quick-witted and never at a loss. As she matured and coarsened – as disappointment, thwarted ambition and worry over money began to sear and ravage her smooth, plump features – her appearance became positively terrifying and her resemblance to Henry VIII in his later years extremely marked. In the picture of her and her second husband, painted shortly

* Henry cut out the descendants of his elder sister, Margaret, Queen of Scotland, (grandmother of Mary, Queen of Scots), for reasons that have never been explained. His war with Scotland and the Franco-Scottish alliance may have been the cause.

before her death, the small, piercing grey eyes have sunk, the reddened swollen cheeks hang in stiff folds, and the expression is one of greedy complacency. It is the face of a woman not so much coldly indifferent to the feelings of others as actively cruel. That these characteristics were shown comparatively early is proved by her attitude towards Jane and her sisters – Katherine was born in 1539 and Mary four years later – whose sex she could not forgive; and no doubt her exacerbation had been increased by the birth of her two half-brothers, of whom the elder succeeded his father as Duke of Suffolk in 1545.

It was inevitable that such a woman should rule, even if discreetly, the husband whom his contemporaries described as 'young, lusty and poor . . . with little or no experience' and 'a senseless creature',[2] although others praised his love of learning, his generosity and his lack of pride. But Dorset was as casually selfish as his wife was cunning and predatory; and their care for their daughters' education sprang, not from aesthetic or intellectual standards, but from this obsession with material advantages and a desire to be in the fashion. These necessities having driven them to seek the society of clever men, he at least, developed the taste for it. Yet there is no indication that either of the Dorsets patronized or frequented such persons until they had children. For some years after he succeeded, Dorset had too many financial worries to think on those lines – he was trying to wrest her property from his widowed mother, whom he treated very badly – and although he had powerful friends and was given many grants and honours by the King, he seems to have mismanaged his affairs.[3] His wife's correspondence shows no interest in culture for its own sake. Her ambitions were political, and her temperament was that of a restless and permanently dissatisfied schemer. She was constantly on the move, in order, it would seem, to keep in touch with her richer friends and her Tudor relations. In any case, a quiet life as the great lady of Bradgate would never have suited her. She was much more fitted than Dorset (although he did his best) to adapt herself to the ever-changing patterns of the religious and political movements controlled by Henry VIII.

In the years immediately before and after Lady Jane's birth these patterns followed a course which was to affect her whole career. Before she was baptized according to the ancient ritual her parents afterwards rejected, while she lay swaddled in her cradle, as she began to learn her alphabet from a coloured horn-book – the principal influences in her life were established under the direction of her great-uncle, that monstrous and incalculable genius who was remaking England and creating the modern State. The destiny of both was bound up with hers; and its divagations must be briefly outlined in so far as they were connected with her early training.

By the end of the 1530s, religio-political dissension had divided the ruling classes into three parties, who were striving with one another. The first was that of the Papalists, who had condemned the nullity suit brought by Henry against Katharine of Aragon and had tried to withstand Parliament's declaration of his supremacy over the Church; this party was in a minority, and before Lady Jane's nursery days were over hardly counted at all. The second, the largest and most powerful, was that of the Henricians; they had approved the nullity suit and the King's second marriage (though a section of them detested Anne Boleyn and helped to bring about her downfall) and were Catholic in everything but obedience to the Pope. The third party, which was beginning to form when Jane was born and was not described as Protestant till her tenth year, became effective as she grew up. It was of course looked on as heretical and criminal by the other two, although Henry himself patronized some of its leaders; it attracted those interested in the New Learning (of which Jane was to become so famous an example), including her tutors; it put her and the Dorsets in touch with continental and Calvinist intellectuals.

Meanwhile the King, who burnt heretics and hanged or beheaded those denying his supremacy, controlled all three parties through subtlety, ruthlessness and prescience. (He had no personal military power; his private army consisted of a hundred Yeomen of the Guard.) A superb statesman and a confident egoist, he knew invariably when to do nothing, when to give way and when to strike; he made no move without the consent of Parliament, and thus always had the State and the country – he remained immensely popular with all but a few of the common people – behind him, on the understanding that he represented both. This attitude was exactly reproduced by Jane during her nine days as Queen of England. The law and the State were all-powerful; subservience to their head was the duty of every Christian, because God had placed the monarch on the throne and supported the regal authority, which was partially delegated by the ruler to nobles and magistrates. Order, obedience and orthodoxy were therefore the slogans of our brutal and turbulent sixteenth-century forebears; but their standards of behaviour did not preclude extraordinary freedom of speech (much disapproved of by foreign visitors), outbreaks of rebellion and what would now be called highly democratic manners on the part of both King and nobles. Henry was much more accessible to his subjects than any other Tudor but Elizabeth, accepted argument and even censure from those who disagreed with him as she never did, and not only tolerated but encouraged the most iconoclastic promoters of the New Learning. He put John Cheke, the friend and adviser of Lady Jane's best-loved tutor, in charge of Prince Edward's education and founded the first professorship of Greek for him at Cambridge.

As the moods and tenses of Henry's policy, both within and without the realm, were reflected in the Dorsets' actions, so Jane's education and point of view were gradually and indirectly affected by such events as the redistribution of monastic lands, the translation of the Bible, the failure of the King's fourth and fifth marriages and the installation of his last wife. Katharine Parr's influence was one of the most important in Jane's life; but she did not come under it till her tenth year. Before then – by the age of five – she had acquired some social experience, and was being trained in public behaviour.

NOTES

1. Nichols, *History of Leicestershire*, vol III, pt 2, p 667; Paget, *Leicestershire*, pp 113–16.

2. *Letters and Papers of Henry VIII* (hereafter cited as *LP*), vol XIII, pt 2, p 280; *Calendar of State Papers, Spanish* (hereafter cited as *Cal SP Spanish*), vol IX, p 489.

3. *LP*, vol XIII, pt 2, p 280.

Chapter 2

The Renaissance Background

HENRY and Frances Dorset were robust and energetic; they spent a great deal of time out of doors and led a healthy, busy life. The routine that suited them was sometimes too strenuous for their daughters, of whom much was required, with the result that both Jane and Katherine were apt to succumb to nervous exhaustion. Mary's birth amounted to a disaster; she was a hump-backed dwarf and very ugly. In earlier days the Dorsets would have been able to dispose of her in a convent; as it was, although she might prove, in spite of her Tudor blood, to be unmarriageable, they did their best for her by giving her the same education as her sisters and took her about with them; but her future was a problem.

Katherine was the beauty of the family; Jane was small, light-haired and neatly made. Her skin was very fair and soon became permanently freckled.[1] This was then considered a serious defect; but nothing was done to remedy it, perhaps because as soon as she passed the first stage of her education she showed herself to be gifted in so many ways that her freckles were overlooked. It became clear that she might grow to emulate, or even surpass that paragon, the Lady Elizabeth, who was her senior by five years. Jane was treated as a princess. She and her sisters took their mother's rank; she was addressed as 'the Lady Jane', met the King's daughters on equal terms and received the same training. Her background and way of life were more luxurious than those of Mary and Elizabeth, who were brought up economically and sometimes in actual hardship. Bradgate was palatial; its interiors reflected the magnificence, and the modernity, of its outward planning. Dorset's father had been one of the pioneers of the new architecture which provided homes built for the enjoyment of wealth and ease, without regard to defence.

Bradgate's focal point was the great hall, which was flanked by wings and placed some two hundred feet behind the towered gateway; it was eighty feet long and its height extended from the bottom to the top of the house. There were wainscoted bay windows (freshly glassed by Henry Dorset) on each side, a musicians' gallery at one end and a dais at the other. Thus, when the family dined in public, they looked down on their guests, who sat at long tables daily set out for some two hundred persons; anyone passing might come to dinner and stay to supper, whether known to their hosts or not. The great hall was warmed by a central fire, the smoke being drawn up through a timbered louver in the roof. The dishes for those sitting below the dais were brought in from the kitchens leading out of the musicians' gallery; another, smaller kitchen lay behind the dais, beyond which were the private apartments, so that the Dorsets could eat by themselves or in company, as they chose. Behind these rooms was the chapel, overlooked by the state bedchamber.[2]

The great hall was ringed by galleries used for indoor exercise and parlour games; these had tapestry hangings and elaborately carved chimney-pieces, so that the Dorset motto, *A Ma Puissance*, supported by two unicorns ermined, armed, and crested and hooped with gold, confronted the spectator at regular intervals. There was little furniture, and few pictures. Here and there carpets were taking the place of scented rushes, and in some rooms gilded clocks displayed figures of men and women set to move to the chimes.

By the time Lady Jane was old enough to dine and sup with her parents, cleanliness and hygiene had been made fashionable by Henry VIII, and the ritual of service at meals was as solemn and complicated as the celebration of Mass. Each course appeared to the sound of trumpets, and all the servants uncovered when the meat was brought in, laying their caps on the sideboards in neat rows. Even in the kitchens anyone found standing with his back to the roast was punished for disrespect to this symbol of bounty and privilege.[3]

Foreigners were amazed by the English passion for meat, which was consumed in great quantities by all but the poorest and accounted, so many declared, for the native unreliability and violence. A passionate, over-fed, hard-drinking, lazy, extravagant people, cutting throats one minute and toasting one another the next, these islanders were hospitable, one French visitor reported ('When they are drunk they will swear blood and death that you must drink all that is in your cup') but mannerless; even in the homes of the great, guests and hosts 'belched at table without reserve or shame'.[4]

There was some reason for this habit, at least in such houses as Bradgate, where the meals achieved terrifying proportions. A nobleman was unworthy of the name whose board was not covered, from end to end, with a vast quantity of dishes for both dinner and supper. (The first might last from eleven till three o'clock, the second from five till eight.) A typical menu consisted of brawn, soup, stewed pheasant, swan, 'subtleties' or sweets (in that order) for the first course. For the second, there was a choice of soups; then came stuffed peacocks, rabbits and egg fritters. The third course started the orgy all over again with almond cream soup, crawfish, baked fruits and more subtleties, followed by the removal of the cloth, washing of hands and serving of caraway-seed wafers and hippocras (hot spiced wine) from trays. In the morning and between meals it was customary to drink beer, nibble saffron buns and tansy cakes (these were made up and fried with breadcrumbs, eggs, cream, nutmeg, ginger, butter and green wheat) and toy with custard pies. There were no forks. The tables were set out with spoons and each person brought a set of knives to meals; with these, and slices of bread – of five sorts, ranging from the purest white manchet to brown barley – they shovelled in the food.[5]

Such arrangements required a code of etiquette which enhanced the formalities of daily life. Lady Jane and her sisters were brought up to eat in silence (without yawning, belching, letting wind or picking their noses) and to select not more than two or three dishes from each course. If they rested after meals, it must be in a chair, or standing against a cupboard, and never

lying down; thus digestion waited on appetite and was preserved for further efforts with the jellies, broths, pancakes and
omelets prepared for nursery fare.[6]

No one ventured to drink water. Ale and beer were served in
silver-bound, earthenware mugs, and wines (of which there was
generally a choice of some thirty varieties) in golden or glass
goblets filled from jewelled and crystal flagons. The gardens
were lavishly stocked with vegetables, fruit and flowers.

Those who, like the Dorsets, had resident physicians and
were able to consult the King's doctors if they wished, were in
fact less fortunate than the poorer classes with their homeo-
pathy and herbal remedies; for English medical standards were
very low. This may partly have accounted for the tuberculosis
which killed Katherine at twenty-eight, and for Jane's nervous
debility. Yet the timetable they began to follow as soon as they
could read – from the age of three or four – was not really
taxing, for they kept early hours and had plenty of sleep. In
country houses the day began with prayers at six, followed by
a breakfast of bread, ale and meat. The young people, having
visited their parents, then worked at Greek and Latin till
dinner-time. Music, modern languages and classical or Biblical
reading lasted till supper; then the girls danced or sat down to
their needlework before going to bed at nine.[7] Once or twice a
week this programme might be set aside for a whole day's hunting, hawking, or an expedition into Leicester, to be entertained
by the mayor and the local gentry.

In her sixth year Lady Jane can be visualized as a girl of
twelve or thirteen would be today, able to interchange a few
simple Latin phrases and to read Coverdale's Bible to herself.
Her nurse, Mrs Ellen, was now her attendant, and helped her
other maids to dress her in clothes which exactly copied those
of her elders. In the 1540s these were very elaborate. Already,
French jewelled hoods, scarlet and purple cloth stockings, bell-
shaped skirts of gold and silver tissue, slashed sleeves nearly
touching the ground and coats of brilliantly coloured satin,
damask and velvet were part of her wardrobe. She learned to
manage the huge overskirts (lined in winter with lynx or sable),
to place her head-dresses so far back that they resembled haloes,

and to keep clean her cambric cuffs, worked with gold thread and caught at the wrists.[8] She was naturally elegant and aware of changes in fashion.

Her favourite hobby was music. She would have liked to practise lute, harp and cithern for more hours than were allowed, and became interested in composition.[9] In her seventh year her first tutor, Dr Harding, began her Greek, Spanish, Italian and French lessons; these had to be fitted in with the writing-master's visits and the time spent learning, not only the Court galliards and pavanes themselves, but the symbolism underlying their movements. It was a full life and, in spite of Frances Dorset's harshness, may have been a happy one. Then, between her eighth and ninth birthdays, the pattern changed. Her parents' plans for her future materialized. She was sent away from home for two years.

ii

The English custom of boarding out young children was as shocking to sixteenth-century foreigners as it is today. A Venetian Ambassador asked one or two noblemen how they had the heart to do such a thing, received rather vague answers about learning manners, and came to the conclusion that they and their wives were in fact too lazy to trouble with the home training of these unfortunate little creatures, many of whom, he noted, might never see their parents again, for the girls married and the boys settled permanently with relatives or friends.[10] This was a misapprehension. In most cases the girls returned after two or three years, and their marriages were arranged at home; they were sent to larger and wealthier establishments so that they might acquire the habits of the fashionable world.

As the Dorsets' position was of the highest, the only way of raising Jane's status was to place her with Queen Katharine Parr. They therefore brought her to the notice of the King as soon as it was feasible; exactly when and how they did so is not recorded.* The Lady Frances, who was frequently at Court,

* Speed, misreading Foxe's famous account of Gardiner's attempt to discredit Katharine Parr with the King, describes 'Lady Jane' carrying the candles before her into the King's apartments and so witness-

made it her business to be on friendly terms with the Queen. By the time Henry VIII's health began to fail, and he withdrew from the bustle of Westminster and Whitehall to the comparative seclusion of Windsor and Hampton Court – between the spring of 1546 and his death in January 1547 – the tenor of life in his palaces had so changed that it would have been difficult, if not impossible, to introduce his great-niece into the Queen's household; for Katharine's responsibilities, which had included her regency during Henry's absence in France, and enforced her constant attendance in his private apartments until a few weeks before his death, when he saw no one but his ministers, would have precluded any other cares. Although it is not clear when Jane left Bradgate, she became known to the Queen, Prince Edward and the Princesses before Henry died. By the time the boy King succeeded and his stepmother had taken up partial residence at Chelsea Palace, Jane had joined her household, and was given precedence of all but her cousins as a princess of the blood.

Her education was thenceforth set in a mould which suited her so well that she never diverged from it. Her establishment in the Queen's circle came at the impressionable age of nine and a half, and its influences prevailed throughout her life. Katharine Parr, one of the most charming and intelligent women of her day, was, temperamentally, the antithesis of Frances Dorset. That Jane became attached to her is obvious, if only because her letters and conversation were to reflect those of her kind and gentle patroness, whose character and career were a typical product of the English Reformation.

When she married Henry VIII in July 1543, Katharine Parr was thirty and had been twice widowed. Her first husband was Lord Borough, her second Lord Latimer. Childless, elegant, wealthy and accomplished, she was an ideal wife and a perfect stepmother. After Lord Latimer's death she was converted to Protestantism, and her house at Wimbledon became the centre

---

ing the scene of Henry's wrath and his wife's self-exculpation. This error has been copied by Miss Strickland and other biographers. As will be seen in early editions of the *Acts and Monuments*, the Queen's attendant on that occasion was the Lady *Lane*, her cousin by marriage.

of an advanced and learned coterie which included Nicholas Udall (later Headmaster of Eton), Coverdale, Cranmer and the ill-fated Anne Askew. During this time Katharine was courted by and fell in love with Thomas Seymour, Lord High Admiral of England and the brother of the late Queen Jane Seymour, Edward's mother. Katharine had been on the point of accepting him when Henry VIII required her hand. So the Admiral, whose career was disastrously intermingled with that of Lady Jane, had to be dismissed. Although he was attached to the Court and well treated by the King, his position and power counted as nothing beside those of his elder brother, Edward Seymour, who, at his nephew's accession, became Duke of Somerset and Protector of the Realm.

Under Somerset's dictatorship, which lasted from 1547 to 1550 – from Jane's eleventh to her fourteenth year – the Protestants, or Reformers, as they preferred to be called, suddenly came into their own, and the pattern of Jane's religious beliefs was accepted and put forward by a number of distinguished and successful persons, including Cheke, Ascham, her future father-in-law John Dudley (later Duke of Northumberland) and several other members of the Council. Although Protestantism then made little or no appeal to the bulk of the English people, its impact on such young and enthusiastic intellectuals as Lady Jane was immediate, violent and lasting. Apart from its denial of certain long-established dogmas, of which the most vital was the Real Presence in the Host, part of its power appears to have lain in its promotion of practical, non-mystical contact with the Deity, comparable to that engendered by seventeenth-century Quakerism. In Jane's spiritual life the question of losing herself in God did not arise. He seems, not so much to have spoken through her, as to have been always available for direct communication and instruction when called upon, with the result that her approach was not ecstatic, but confident – although humble – and serene. There was no dark night of the soul for persons of her temperament and training, and, once she had been taught what to do, little need to consult those more experienced than herself as to how to get in touch with her Creator, although she pursued discussion and analysis on the subject by correspondence. The process of establishing the divine nearness was comparatively simple, requiring no intermediary. Cheke describes it in a letter written in 1549 to an anonymous woman friend. 'In hearing the word of God,' he says, 'whether it be by the voice of others pronouncing *or by yourself reading*, you are ever to think that God speaketh to you ... You are to remember that you speak to God ... You walk in the eye and sight of God ... When you speak to God, know that you speak to Him who understandeth the bottom of your heart.'[11]

This attitude was apt to breed a certain arrogance (very marked in Lady Jane), contempt for and horror of those who preferred the old ways, and, in the case of most young persons brought up as she was on the classics – Ascham considered them next to the Bible in importance – instinctive association of the Platonic theories with the Protestant outlook. The *Phaedo* became Jane's favourite Dialogue after she left Katharine Parr's circle; some of its key passages exactly reflect her and her contemporaries' opinions about death, as expressed by Socrates before taking the hemlock from the hands of the executioner. 'I ought to be grieved at death,' he is reported to have said, 'if I were not persuaded ... that I am going to other gods who are wise and good ... and therefore I do not grieve ... The real philosopher has reason to be of good cheer when he is about to die ... After death he may be able to obtain the greatest good in the other world ... When I come to the end of my journey I shall obtain that which has been the pursuit of my life.'[12]

This immunity from terror was strengthened by the vision – then entertained by all sincerely religious persons of whatever creed – of an absolutely concrete heaven, as described in the prophecies of Isaiah and the Revelation of St John the Divine. There was hell too, of course; but, for the Protestants, no disagreeable interval of purgatory. And for such as Jane, the temptations to stray from righteousness and thus risk damnation were very few; indeed, they hardly occurred. Her interests were aesthetic and literary; she was neither worldly, grasping nor carnally minded. All she had to do therefore, in order to prepare for Paradise, was to abjure and, when occasion required, to inveigh against the idolatry of the Mass – that was not difficult, because everyone in her circle, her parents included, did so – and follow the teachings of those she admired most, while regarding herself as a sinner who could yet count on admittance to the celestial city. There, according to Thomas Becon, another contemporary, 'Your joy, your gladness, your mirth shall be perpetual. All the pleasure of this world compared to the least joy of heaven is nothing ... Ye shall receive the crown of life, which the Lord hath promised to them that love Him ... an incorruptible crown of glory.'[13]

With this ineffable rapture ahead and the newly discovered intoxication of philosophic inquiry to feed on while waiting for it, mundane pleasures were easily rejected. It was necessary, naturally, for older persons such as Katharine Parr to deprecate past error. This she did in a book published in 1548, *The Lamentations of a Sinner*, which had a preface by the invaluable and promising young William Cecil, then Somerset's private secretary. It sold well, perhaps because it reproduced, in a rather commonplace style, the Protestant attitude towards the old and the new faiths.

So the education of this remarkable girl intensified its pressure, hardening and crystallizing her outlook. Demure, retiring but not shy, Lady Jane listened and learned, finding the happiness and warmth in the Queen Dowager's company she had never been given at home. Then the pleasant rhythms of life at Chelsea and Whitehall – where Katharine had a suite of rooms next to the King's private apartments[14] – were suddenly destroyed. Intrigue and passion broke up the household; and at the age of eleven Jane lost the first person who had ever been kind to her.

NOTES

1. Davey, *Life and Times of Lady Jane Grey*.
2. Paget, *Leicestershire*, pp 113–16; Nichols, *History of Leicestershire*, vol IV, p 666; Salzmann, *England in Tudor Times*, p 86.
3. Ibid.

4. *Antiquarian Repertory*, vol IV, pp 503–10.

5. Furnivall, *Early English Meals and Manners*, pp 48, 94, 128–9.

6. Ibid.

7. Ibid.

8. Laver, *Early Tudor Costume*, pp 7–8.

9. Strype, *Life of Aylmer*, pp 195–6.

10. *Calendar of State Papers, Venetian* (hereafter cited as *Cal SP Venetian*), vol IV, p 1672.

11. Harington, *Nugae Antiquae*, vol II, pp 175–87.

12. Jowett's translation.

13. Becon, *Early Works*, p 55.

14. Rapin de Thoyras, *History of England*, vol VII, p 28.

Chapter 3

The Sale of Lady Jane

A F E W weeks after the death of Henry VIII the Lord Admiral reappeared in Katharine Parr's life. Very soon he was visiting her secretly, at Whitehall and in her country palace of Chelsea. Jane was now a member of the Court circle; a silent, background figure, she yet had importance, not only because of her status but because her intellectual powers were already apparent. She was considered extraordinarily advanced for her age. No one then, least of all the King's tutors, would have admitted that she surpassed him; her development shows that she did, and also that she might be a match for him in more than one sense.

It now occurred to the Admiral that he was the very person to arrange an alliance between the cousins. His doing so would diminish the prestige of the Protector, who was carrying out the late King's policy of obtaining a French or Spanish princess for his nephew. Seymour consulted Dorset, and they agreed to work together on the scheme; meanwhile, the Admiral pursued a number of his own. The first was to ruin the Protector, of whom he was bitterly jealous: the second to find an heiress for himself. He proposed marriage – in what order is not clear – to Anne of Cleves, the Duchess of Richmond (widow of Henry VIII's bastard son, and the Duke of Norfolk's only daughter), the Princesses Mary and Elizabeth, and Katharine Parr. Katharine's love for him had never died, and she encouraged his advances, although with many qualms. The Admiral then set about subjugating the King – an easy matter, for Somerset was over-strict with him, and his tutors, although devoted, were too disciplinary – and began to form a party against his brother. So Jane was plunged in the midst of a Palace intrigue spun round herself, the Queen Dowager and the boy King by

Seymour and his allies, of whom the principal was her own father.[1]

Thomas Seymour was high-spirited, violent, bold and unscrupulous – in fact, the essentially masculine type of scoundrel, whose goods glitter in the shop window and who can cajole, persuade and even fascinate, until he is seen through, when he at once moves on to the next victim. To be successful, such persons must have good looks, accomplishments and immense physical vitality. The Admiral had all these, in addition to many of the graces, without the qualities, of a fine gentleman. Tall, athletic, dashing, richly bearded and magnificently dressed, he was the perfect *faux bonhomme*, the classic cad, to whom women and young people are immediately attracted, and whom most men despise after a short acquaintance. A loyal contemporary describes him as 'hardy, wise and liberal', adding that 'he, through malice, went to pot'.[2] 'There is something about him' is what his supporters would say now; and that vague description must suffice, because only one of those he took by storm was able to define, and then inadequately, the nature of his power. 'A man of much wit and little judgement', was the sixteen-year-old Elizabeth's summing-up. The Admiral's boisterous humour – a message to Elizabeth asking 'if her great buttocks were grown any less or no'[3] is a fair example – was combined with an instinctive realization of what most people wanted; if it suited him, he provided it. To Edward VI, who complained that his elder uncle kept him short of ready cash, he gave presents of money; he made Katharine feel both royal and desirable by the mingled courtliness and fervour of his approach; he excited Elizabeth by his romping sexuality: and for Lady Jane, who had never known parental love, he seems to have produced the warmth and gaiety, perhaps even the spoiling ways, of an indulgent uncle. Edward, less intellectually advanced but more acute in his judgement of people than his cousin, soon perceived the Admiral's falsity; Jane did not, as will presently appear; but then her circumstances made her more accessible to Seymour's appeal, for Edward had been surrounded by adoring relatives and attendants since his birth, and everything he did and said was ecstatically received.

When Jane had been with the Queen Dowager for some months, Dorset, who seems to have been pushing his interests from his London house, began to grow impatient; and, as so often happened, he was unable to get in touch with the Admiral. He talked of removing Jane from his household if nothing were done about her marriage. At last Seymour sent one of his gentlemen, Harington (father of the author, Sir John, who was knighted under Elizabeth) to reassure him. 'Be contented,' said Harington, 'that your daughter Jane shall be with the Admiral. I dare assure you he will find the means she shall be placed in marriage much to your comfort.' 'With whom will he match her?' said Dorset suspiciously. 'Marry,' exclaimed Harington, 'I doubt not but you shall see him marry her to the King. And fear you not,' he added, as Dorset still looked doubtful, 'but he will bring it to pass, and then shall you be able to help all the friends you have.'[4]

Still nothing happened. Finally Dorset went to the Admiral's house in Seymour Place and had a talk with him in the garden, out of the hearing of the servants. Seymour was full of promises and schemes; but if Dorset was so foolish as to remove the Lady Jane, they would never be realized. He must have her guardianship; and he was willing to pay for it. What Dorset afterwards described as 'certain covenants' were then agreed upon; they resulted in Seymour's paying Dorset some hundreds on account of the £2,000 that would be his if Jane was officially contracted to the King. Later on Seymour said to Harington, 'My Lord Marquess is cold about my guardianship of the Lady Jane. She is as handsome a lady,' he went on expansively, 'as any in England, and she might be wife to any prince in Christendom. If the King's Majesty, when he comes of age, would marry within the realm, he would wish it,' he added rather vaguely, thus making it clear to Harington that he had taken no practical steps about the alliance – and indeed, this was not possible, for the Protector, as Edward's Governor, was in absolute control. It would not do for Dorset to know this, however. A few days later Seymour told Harington that he had thought better of the marriage plan, as being rather dangerous. He continued to make 'fair promises' to Dorset, and Lady Jane stayed on; there were plenty of people in the Queen's household who would have repeated their master's compliments; and Jane may have heard them from himself.

Till she came under the Queen Dowager's care Jane had been neither praised nor loved. (The famous eulogies of Ascham and others were to come.) Now her situation changed. Katharine grew very fond of her; she and Edward, exactly of an age and at the same point in their studies, found many tastes in common; and as the rumours of her being married to him began to spread, she received a great deal of admiration and flattery. This atmosphere of adulation may have been enhanced by the fact that the Protector, from whom his brother's schemes had so far been concealed, was considering a marriage between Jane and his eldest son, Lord Hertford, a handsome lad of fourteen. So it may be concluded that the Lady Jane's talents and graces were much discussed, to the exclusion indeed of those of Mary and Elizabeth. Sir John Hayward, writing a hundred years later, yet reflects the contemporary attitude towards her at this time. She had, he says, 'most rare and incomparable perfections; for besides her excellent beauty, adorned with all variety of virtues, as a clear sky with stars, as a princely diadem with jewels, she was most dear to the King, both in regard of her religion [Edward was an advanced Protestant] . . . and of her knowledge'.[5] Bishop Bale, who knew the King well and Jane hardly at all, believed that Edward wanted to marry her. The references to marriage in Edward's diary contradict this view. His mind was set, either on a continental alliance or on his father's plan of contracting him to the five-year-old Queen of Scots; in any case, he desired, in his own phrase, 'a well stuffed and jewelled' bride. The fact that his cousin had a passion, according to Bale, 'for literature and the elegant arts'[6] weighed less with the practical Edward than the political and material assets of the Princess Elisabeth of France, for whom the Council was negotiating.

As these two fair, slight, composed children got to know one another, ceremony never relaxed. When Jane entered her cousin's presence, whether publicly or otherwise, she curtsied three times and knelt when he addressed her. If they settled down for a talk or a game of cards, she waited for his permission to sit, and then did so on a cushion or a stool. When he dismissed her she knelt again to kiss his hand, walked backwards from the room and curtsied at the door, which was opened for her by his pages. Two or more ladies attended her at the whole interview, standing in the background or waiting in the antechamber for as long as His Majesty chose to remain with their mistress.[7]

Meanwhile Katharine was persuaded by the Admiral to marry him secretly. They confided in the King, whose approval and support would protect them from the wrath of Somerset and the Privy Council. By the end of May 1547 all was known, and the Protector, although much displeased, had forgiven his brother. A year passed happily and uneventfully for Jane, perhaps because Seymour's plans for her marriage to his nephew did not materialize, and she moved with the Queen Dowager from one splendid palace to another – Hanworth, Chelsea, Whitehall. In the summer of 1548 she retired with Katharine to the Admiral's property of Sudeley Castle in Gloucestershire. There the Queen gave birth to a daughter and died eight days afterwards of puerperal fever. Then the clouds began to gather round Lady Jane.

For several months the Admiral had ceased to make any pretence of affection for the wife who had risked so much for him. His behaviour to the Princess Elizabeth – and her reception of it – had ended in her leaving his household for one of her own. As Katharine lay dying she came out of her delirium to reproach him. 'I am not well handled,' she whispered to the gentlewoman nearest her, 'for those that be about me care not for me, but stand laughing at my grief, and the more good I will to them, the less good they will to me'. 'Why, sweetheart,' said Seymour in his jolly way, 'I would you no hurt.' 'No, my lord? I think so,' she replied, adding, 'but, my lord, you have given me many shrewd taunts'. And then, falling again into confusion, she began to mutter about the doctor – why had my lord not let him stay with her? – and her will. Trying to soothe her, Seymour lay down on the bed beside her – perhaps even his shrivelled heart was touched – and her ladies were dis-

missed. Three days later she was dead, and he had the satis-
faction of knowing that the poor woman had not only left him
all her possessions, but 'wished that they had been a thousand
times more than they were'.[8] So did the Admiral; for he was
always short of money, and now his situation had become desperate. He was no nearer his combined scheme of ousting the
Protector and marrying Lady Jane to the King. He left
Gloucestershire before the funeral, hurrying back to London to
get in touch with Edward, and Jane was chief mourner at the
ceremonies in the Chapel of Sudeley Castle.

Instructions were sent from Whitehall that Her Majesty's
obsequies were to be of the kind befitting the widow of a great
king, and so the chapel was transformed by multicoloured
heraldic banners superimposed on the black cloth covering the
walls; altar-rails and cushions were similarly draped. At two
o'clock the procession began with a party of heralds and ushers
in black surcoats. The coffin was carried in by six gentlemen in
hooded gowns, followed by torch-bearers. Then, under the
royal canopy of State embroidered with the arms of the Tudors
and the Seymours, the diminutive figure of the Lady Jane
appeared, walking alone, in deepest black; her long train of
purple velvet was borne up by one of her ladies, a girl of about
her own age. The rest of the household came after, proceeding
in pairs.[9]

The service was strictly Protestant: a demonstration of the
new order. Psalms were sung in English, the lessons read in
Coverdale's translation. He himself preached the sermon,
taking occasion to delare, 'None here shall think that the offer-
ing has done anything to appease [plead for] the dead, but
[it is] for the poor only. And also the lights are for the honour
of the person.'[10]

So Queen Katharine's almoner and protégé condemned the
ancient ways; but this was still an age of superstition, one rich
in portents, omens and premonitions: when signs and wonders,
good and evil spirits, rose at the conjuration of wizards and
prophets. Yet five years later, as a selected party of spectators
walked away from the dripping scaffold on Tower Green, no
one remarked that the first public appearance of the nine days'

Queen had shown her muffled in the trappings of woe, and encompassed by the emblems of mortality.

ii

As soon as he heard of the Queen Dowager's death, Dorset sent for Lady Jane to his London house, and Seymour seemed rather relieved than otherwise that she should go. At any rate, he consented to her departure, and she remained with her parents for a little while. The letters that passed between them and the Admiral during the next few weeks make it clear that they had perceived a change in her. She was no longer the docile, quiet little creature they had known at Bradgate. Dorset did not like this development, and neither did his wife; what concerned them much more, however, was the Admiral's failure to arrange her marriage, and they decided to cut their losses and remove her permanently from his charge. Seymour then visited them and insisted that all would yet be well, if they would let her come back to him. 'As he would have no nay,' said Dorset afterwards, 'we were contented she again return to his house,' and Lady Jane and her attendants accompanied the Admiral to Hanworth, escorted by Harington, to whom Seymour said, 'Lady Jane should not be married until such time as she should be able to bear a child, and her husband to get one,' thus indicating that he was going to keep her indefinitely while doing nothing about her marriage.[11] She was an asset; her presence in his household raised his status. To Parry, Princess Elizabeth's treasurer, he confided a secondary scheme. 'There hath been a tale of late,' he said, 'they say now I shall marry my Lady Jane,' adding with his great laugh, 'I tell you this but merrily – merrily.'[12]

Seymour might have succeeded in putting off Dorset; his wife was not so easily satisfied. She began to worry too, about her daughter's position – who was chaperoning her? Seymour answered her objections in a soothing letter to her husband.

His great loss, he began, had given him the feeling that he must alter his way of life, but now, 'being better advised … I find indeed that with God's help I shall right well be able to hold together my household.' He was keeping on all his wife's maids, and could therefore provide suitable attendants for Lady Jane. Also, his mother, old Lady Seymour, had arrived, 'who will, I doubt not, be as dear to me as to [Jane], as though she were her own daughter. And for my own part,' he concluded, 'I shall be her half father, and more; and all that be in my household shall be as diligent about her as yourself would wish.' He added that he and the Dorsets must meet to discuss the matter as soon as he returned from Court.[13]

When they did so, Seymour renewed his promises. 'I will marry her to the King's Majesty,' he declared. 'If I might get the King at liberty –' he meant out of Somerset's care – 'I dare warrant you he shall marry her. My lady should let her come to me' – that is, permanently.

At first Dorset did not wish to leave Jane with the Admiral; then he hesitated. At last Frances Dorset wrote, thanking Seymour for his offer. They would continue to take his advice about Jane's future – ie, her marriage with the King; but he must trust her as 'his good sister', to know what was best for their own child.

Once more the Admiral had to plead for Jane's guardianship. Dorset replied with a description of her development. She was too young, he said, to be away from home. Furthermore, 'she shall hardly rule herself as yet without a guide, *lest she should, for lack of a bridle, take too much the head*, and conceive such opinion of herself that all such behaviour as she hath heretofore learned, by the Queen's and your most wholesome instructions, should either be quenched in her, or at the least, much diminished.' In fact, Dorset thought that Jane had been spoilt and was becoming unmanageable. He added that she would 'most easily be ruled and framed towards virtue ... by the eye and oversight of my wife ... My meaning herein is not to withdraw any part of my promise to you for her bestowing [in marriage] only I seek in these her young years ... the addressing of her mind to humility, soberness and obedience.' He again stressed the necessity of her mother's influence, and concluded with assurances of loyalty and friendship.[14]

It seems that Lady Jane had changed, from the Dorsets' point of view, for the worse; perhaps the strength of character which was to surprise so many was now apparent beneath her quiet exterior. Again, she returned to her parents; and before they were again persuaded by Harington and Seymour to give her up, she herself wrote to the Admiral, formally, as the occasion required; yet beneath the stiff phrases the desire for his company is clearly seen.

After thanking him for his letters to her, she dwelt on his 'great goodness' towards herself. 'I cannot by any means be able to recompense the least part thereof,' she continued, 'and purposed to write a few rude lines unto your Lordship rather as a token ... Like as you have been to me a loving and kind father, so I shall be always ready to obey your goodly monitions and good instructions, as becometh one upon whom you have heaped so many benefits ... Your humble servant during my life, Jane Grey. To the right honourable and my singular good lord, the Lord Admiral, give these.'[15]

She returned to the Admiral's care at about the time of her twelfth birthday. Before she did so Dorset received another five hundred pounds. No bond, said Seymour, was required; the Lady Jane herself should be his gauge.[16]

The Dorsets were now committed to the Admiral's cause; they found themselves involved in a conspiracy to overthrow the government and seize the person of the King. Among the plotters was Sir William Sherington, Master of the Mint, who by issuing worthless coins supplied some of the funds; another was the late Queen's brother, William Parr, now Marquess of Northampton. Cheke was bribed; Edward was still receiving money from the Admiral through one of his gentlemen in Seymour's pay; and the Earl of Rutland had promised his support.

Northampton was one of the first to see that Seymour's schemes might fail. Walking in the gallery of the Admiral's London house, he tried to warn him. 'There will be much ado,' said the Admiral defiantly, 'for my Lady Jane. My Lord Protector and my Lady Somerset will do what they can to obtain her of my Lord Marquess Dorset for my Lord of Hertford. But they shall not prevail therein,' he went on, 'for my Lord Marquess hath given her wholly to me, upon certain covenants that are between us two.' 'What shall you do,' asked Northampton, who knew Dorset's unreliable ways, 'if my Lord Protector, handling my Lord Dorset gently, should obtain his goodwill?' 'I will never consent thereto,' was the haughty answer. Northampton then taxed Seymour with his aspirations to the Princess Elizabeth's hand. The Admiral denied that he had ever courted her, and was not believed. To Sherington he announced, 'For her qualities and virtue [the Lady Jane] is a fit marriage for the King. I would rather the King should marry her than my Lord Protector's daughter.'[17] (The reference was to another Lady Jane, who was to die unmarried some fifteen years later.)

Dorset was more sanguine about Jane's prospects. 'Except the King's Majesty only,' he said to Seymour, 'I will spend my life and blood in your part against all men.'[18] The Admiral took him up on this point, for he was now determined to raise the country against his brother – why did not Dorset join him? He might begin, Seymour went on, by turning his Warwickshire property into a stronghold for men and arms. Dorset replied that he could not afford to do so. 'I take the provision that I have at Bradgate,' was all he would say. 'Trust not too much to the gentlemen,' Seymour urged, 'for they have somewhat to lose – but I will rather advise you to make much of the head yeomen. Go to their houses, now to one, now to another, carrying with you a flagon of wine, and a pasty of venison – and use a familiarity with them, for so shall you cause them to love you.'[19]

Dorset did not follow this advice, preferring to fall back on the Protector's half-promise – which had been concealed from Seymour – that Lord Hertford should marry Jane. 'I think it is not meet to be written,' he told Somerset, adding cryptically, 'but I shall at all times avouch my saying.'[20]

Between the autumn of 1548 and January of the following year the Admiral's schemes became more daring and widespread. He ignored all warnings, including those of his friends on the Privy Council. 'Beware what you are doing,' said Wriothesley, one of the most influential. 'It were better for you if you had never been born, nay, that you were burnt quick alive, than that you should attempt it.' Meanwhile Seymour would not accept the fact that Edward had seen through him; it was his brother's fault that he could not obtain access to His Majesty. By this time Sir William Sherington had collected £10,000 and the rising was planned – in the Admiral's brain, at least. Still nothing happened; no one would join him in the first move. At last, maddened by the King's withdrawal and his allies' pusillanimity, Seymour, armed with a pistol and accompanied by two servants, broke into Edward's bedchamber through the Privy Garden, presumably with the intent to kidnap him. The King's little dog sprang up, barking, and Seymour shot it. The report roused the household. He was seized, attainted, and executed a few weeks later. As soon as he was arrested the Dorsets removed Lady Jane to Bradgate, having supplied the Privy Council with all the evidence they needed and thus exculpating themselves.

For the next three years Jane remained with her parents. In their eyes she was now a symbol of failure and of wasted effort – and they treated her accordingly.

NOTES

1. Chapman, *The Last Tudor King*, chaps VI, VII.
2. *The Legend of Sir Nicholas Throckmorton*, ed Nichols, p 17.
3. *Burleigh State Papers*, ed Haynes, p 98.
4. Tytler, *England under the Reigns of Edward VI and Mary*, vol I, pp 137–8; Haynes, p 82.
5. Hayward, *Life of Edward VI*, p 421.
6. Nichols, *History of Leicestershire*, vol III, p 666.
7. Raumer, vol II, p 71.
8. Strickland, *Lives of the Queens of England*, vol II, pp 460–61.
9. *Archaeologia*, vol V, pp 234–6.
10. Ibid.
11. Tytler, vol I, pp 137–8; Haynes, p 93.
12. Ibid.
13. Ibid.
14. Ibid, p 78.
15. Tytler, vol I, p 132.

16. Haynes, p 76.
17. Ibid, p 80.
18. Ibid, p 76.
19. Ibid.
20. Ibid.

Chapter 4

The Intellectual and Spiritual Life

IN the winter of 1550, when Lady Jane had been living at home for a year, Roger Ascham's tutorship of the Princess Elizabeth came to an end, and he was sent to the Low Countries as secretary to Sir Richard Morrison, Edward VI's Ambassador to Charles V. Ascham was thirty-five, and his book *Toxophilus* (a work on archery, full of personal reminiscences and anecdotes), published five years earlier, had made his name in Protestant and intellectual circles. Among his many friends were Haddon, now the Dorsets' chaplain, and Aylmer, their daughters' new tutor. Before leaving England, Ascham accepted an invitation to stay at Bradgate.

Riding across the park, he observed that the Dorsets and their household were out hunting. In need of a rest after his journey, he went on to the house and asked if anyone – presumably he meant Haddon or Aylmer – was at home. Only my Lady Jane was within doors, he was told; and he was ushered into her room.

Then followed one of the most famous conversations in English history, recorded by Ascham in the vivid, informal style which made his work so popular. He incorporated his account into his most celebrated book, *The Schoolmaster*, posthumously published in 1570; it reads as if he noted down what Jane said soon after they parted. 'It was the last time,' he added, 'I ever beheld that sweet and noble lady.' He used their talk to illustrate one of his favourite themes, which was that learning should be made easy and agreeable and that the cruel punishments then and long afterwards part of the curriculum should be discarded.

After the usual courtesies had been exchanged Ascham noticed that Lady Jane was reading the *Phaedo* of Plato, 'with as much delight as if it had been a merry tale of Boccaccio'. 'Why, Madam,' he asked, 'do you relinquish such pastime as going into the park?'

She smiled. 'I wis all their sport is but a shadow to that pleasure I find in Plato,' she said. As Ascham seemed rather taken aback, she went on, 'Alas! good folk, they never felt what pleasure means.' 'And how attained you, Madam,' Ascham asked, 'to this true knowledge of pleasure? And what did chiefly allure you to it, seeing that few women and not many men have arrived at it?'

Ascham's capacity for drawing people out had made itself felt when he and Jane met at Whitehall. Now she, who had few confidants, found the perfect listener. She spoke with a freedom and articulateness which were already characteristic – and at considerable length. 'I will tell you,' she began, 'and tell you a truth which perchance you will marvel at. One of the greatest benefits that ever God gave me is that He sent me, with sharp, severe parents, so gentle a schoolmaster. When I am in presence of either father or mother, whether I speak, keep silence, sit, stand or go, eat, drink, be merry or sad, be sewing, playing, dancing or doing anything else, I must do it, as it were, in such weight, measure and number, even as perfectly as God made the world – or else I am so sharply taunted, so cruelly threatened, yea, presented sometimes with pinches, nips and bobs [blows] and other ways – which I will not name for the honour I bear them – so without measure misordered, *that I think myself in hell* – till the time comes when I must go to Mr Aylmer, who teacheth me so gently, so pleasantly, with such fair allurements to learning, that I think all the time nothing whiles I am with him.'

Ascham made no comment – perhaps he was too much amazed to do so – and the thirteen-year-old victim went on, 'And when I am called from him I fall on weeping, because whatever I do else but learning is full of great trouble, and whole misliking unto me. And thus –' she concluded – 'my book hath been so much my pleasure, and bringeth daily to me more pleasure – and more – that in respect of it, all other pleasures, in very deed, be but trifles and troubles to me.'[1]

For four hundred years Lady Jane's celebrated attack on her
parents has been used, first to illustrate her superlatively intellectual standards – which were, in fact, only a little higher than
those of several other young women in her circle – and secondly
as an example of the harshness shown by sixteenth-century
parents towards their children. One aspect of it has been entirely ignored, and should now be visualized. What had she
done – or not done – to arouse this brutality? In that age,
young people of both sexes and all classes were flogged and
knocked about, either for neglecting their lessons, or for dis-
obedience, or for lapses of manners. Lady Jane could never
have been guilty of laziness: by her own and her tutors' show-
ing, her lessons absorbed her; she had been carefully trained at
home and by Queen Katharine Parr in the social graces; and
her piety demanded submission to her elders. Her vehement
condemnation of the Dorsets makes it clear that she was a
burden to them, one they so bitterly resented as to be unable to
let the smallest deviation pass without turning upon her in an
access of irritation. (There is no record of their having treated
her sisters in this way.) Apart from the fact that the plans for
her marriage with the King were held up – not irrecoverably,
for they were still being talked of – in what other ways did she
remind them, if only tacitly, that their ambitions were frus-
trated (perhaps even contemptible) and their schemes
destroyed? The answer seems to lie in Dorset's letter to the
Admiral, written the year before Ascham's visit to Bradgate.
'She should, for lack of a bridle, take too much the head ... I
seek ... the addressing of her mind to humility, soberness and
obedience.' Was he now seeking it in vain?

Three years later, this young girl's command of her situation
and her refusal to give in over matters of principle showed an
endemic resistance to pressure; and this resistance, not un-
naturally regarded by her parents as obstinate and undutiful,
was already making itself felt. One fault in 'sewing, playing,
dancing or doing anything else' was greeted with taunts, curses
and blows – why? Frances Dorset was a hard, imperious
woman, who required, as most mothers then did, absolute subservience from her children; but her husband was noted for his

easy-going ways, his gaiety and his good humour. Yet he also let Jane feel the weight of his hand, criticizing and censuring her, till she thought herself in hell in his company.

Lady Jane gave Ascham a horrible picture of her home life; yet her contribution to those ugly scenes of pinching, beating – and worse treatment, which she could not bring herself to describe – must be considered. The Dorsets, although savagely selfish, were not sadistic: nor were they stupid; and as far as the failure of her marriage was concerned, they knew her to be blameless. She may however have deepened a split in the household of which Ascham knew nothing. At this time Haddon and Aylmer were siding together against their employers about a private matter, and the Dorsets deeply resented their interference: but they were too valuable to be dismissed. So the dispute went on, and Lady Jane, who modelled her conduct on her tutor's, must have allied herself with him against her parents.

The Dorsets were great gamblers, and all the members of their household followed their example. Haddon and Aylmer protested in vain; and the quarrel continued as long as they remained under the Marquess' roof, that is, for some three years.[2] Lady Jane, whose instinct was to put herself in the right – in this case, to reject any form of dissipation – was at one with Aylmer and Haddon.

Furthermore, although she had been brought up in a sporting, games-playing family, all her tastes lay in the opposite direction; reading, writing, music, were her passion. It may be that her withdrawal from outdoor pursuits, emphasized by the force of her personality and her powers of self-expression, was neither forgiven nor forgotten. Her way of life, admirable in the eyes of Ascham and his friends, was not only antipathetic to the Dorsets, but in itself an act of defiance. They might have softened her resistance by persuasion, or by an appeal to the affections (Katharine Parr would certainly have done so); but they would not stoop to the first and were incapable of the second. As they disliked and abused her, so she avoided them and shut herself up with her books. As their annoyance increased, so did her determination, and her dependence on the learning and culture which they had provided because it was customary and, in a purely worldly sense, beneficial. In their circle, knowledge and accomplishments were essential, the signs of privilege and wealth. Jane desired them for themselves, to the exclusion of other amusements and hobbies. 'All other pleasures, in very deed, be but trifles and troubles to me.' And she could afford to pity those who did not agree with her. 'Alas! good folk, they never felt what pleasure means.' So, unknown to herself, she was storing up strength for a series of hideous ordeals and making use, as it were, of her parents' coldness and cruelty.

That a clever girl of thirteen should be fascinated by philosophic inquiry, and especially by that branch dealing with the spiritual life, was very natural, however surprising it may have seemed to later generations and even to the middle-aged Ascham, many of whose first pupils had no doubt preferred the 'merry tales' of Boccaccio to the Platonic Dialogues. Lady Jane's generation and type were not interested in narrative, or in personalities. Analysis, speculation (particularly on theological lines) and comparison of the classic with the Christian theories about survival after death and the way to salvation were, to her, more absorbing and satisfying than any relation of fact, or of fancy; they led into, and could be linked up with, the basis of her whole existence in this world and the next. She studied her faith, first through the Bible and then through the works of the Fathers. Compared with these, the history of her own country, in which she was to play so brief and tragic a part, appeared shadowy, transient and trivial, quite apart from the fact that in her day it was neither skilfully presented nor intellectually acceptable. The chronicles of Polydore Vergil and Hall, or Berners' translations of Froissart, so interesting to later generations, must have seemed childish and negligible to those accustomed to the sophisticated eloquence of Demosthenes, Isocrates and Plato, and the breath-taking splendour of the *Aeneid*. Contemplation of the soul and of eternity, the defeat of Popery, the propagation and justification of 'pure' religion were combined with the thrilling pursuit of knowledge for its own sake, in Greek, Latin, Hebrew and modern tongues, and every moment not spent on them was time wasted. English literature, then, provided no books that persons of Lady Jane's calibre could have enjoyed, as is shown by the catalogue of Edward VI's library, which contained nothing by Chaucer or Malory, and no translations of the medieval and continental romances that had delighted pre-Reformation readers.

To set down Lady Jane and her co-equals as precocious prigs and dry-as-dust scholars would be unwise; such a judgement precludes all awareness of or sympathy with their world. Their standards and tastes, deriving from such iconoclastic thinkers and humanists as Erasmus and Sir Thomas More, had led them to a culture never yet equalled in the history of mankind, that of ancient Greece and Italy. To young people, discovery, of whatever nature, is exciting; and the teachers patronized by the Tudors and the Dorsets had the gift of making it more so. They followed Sir Thomas Elyot's precept, that children should not be 'enforced by violence to learn ... but sweetly allured thereto with praises ... and pretty gifts'.[3] They made the early stages of learning easy by surrounding their pupils with educated attendants who, conversing in Greek, Latin, French and Italian, instructed them aurally, before they could read, thus eliminating much drudgery later on.

In fact, Lady Jane's cultural background was dazzling, and her appreciation of it limitless and constant. She can hardly be censured for preferring that rich feast and entrancing intercourse to the crude fare and political and social chit-chat provided by parents who abused and ill-treated her. She 'fell on weeping' when called away from Aylmer because he was spirited, witty, highly unconventional and deeply affectionate: the sort of person who utters the unexpected thought, and speaks his mind without regard to consequences. Beginning his career as a servant in Dorset's household, he went to Cambridge, took orders and returned to Bradgate shortly after getting in touch with the group of Calvinist divines whose books and letters became another of Jane's interests. A small, energetic, bustling man, he threw himself into whatever he did with engaging eagerness, had a fund of amusing stories and was a great patriot. ('God is an Englishman,' he used to say.) He was

fond of bowling, and would run after his bowl with cries of
'Rub, rub, rub!', exclaiming 'The devil go with it!' in the event
of failure.[4] He had loved Jane since her infancy, and was no
doubt very sorry for her when she returned home after the
Admiral's execution.

ii

The disadvantages of Lady Jane's upbringing became apparent
during the years that followed Ascham's visit. Through him,
Aylmer and Haddon, she began to correspond with Bucer,
Bullinger, Ulmis and other German Calvinist and Zwinglian
ministers, some of whom had lectured at Cambridge and were
now her father's pensioners. Their first letters were to Dorset;
but somehow, he was always occupied, or away; and so his
eldest daughter took his place.

It was still hoped and believed by all these divines that Jane's
marriage with the King would eventually be brought about
(that His Majesty should take a Popish princess to his bed was
unthinkable) and so they wrote to her as to a future Queen, in
ecstatic admiration. She replied, deprecating her intellectual
unworthiness, but in the same strain. The Zürich Letters, as
they came to be called, describe a mutual admiration society
revolving round a lonely girl of fourteen, whose principal outlet was this heady yet esoteric interchange, inaugurated by
Ascham in one of his first letters to Aylmer. In a mingling of
Greek and Latin he addresses Jane and Aylmer simultaneously.
'O! Good God! what a divine maid, diligently reading ... the
divine *Phaedo* ... In this respect you are to be reckoned happier
than that by both father and mother you derive your stock from
kings and queens.' He goes on, '*Elmarum meum felicissimum!*
to whose lot it falls to have such a scholar, and you, Madam,
how fortunate in such a master – all joy to you both.' He then
suggested that Jane should write to him and to some of his
friends in Greek.[5]

The correspondence opens with a note in Latin from Dorset
to Bullinger, thanking him for a letter and a book. He has been
much occupied with State business, but is fervent for the true

religion. 'I am much indebted to you on my daughter's account, for having exhorted her in your godly letters to ... the study of the Scriptures, purity of manners and innocence of life.'[6]

Lady Jane's letters, written in Latin, with here and there a Greek phrase, show the intoxication of the neophyte, and are of inordinate length. '*Vir ornatissime!*' she begins to Bullinger, 'I give you unceasing thanks, and shall do as long as I live ... I am unworthy of the correspondence of so distinguished a personage ... Your writings are ... not merely topics for amusement, but pious and divine thoughts for instruction, admonition and counsel ... Oh! happy me, to be possessed of so wise a friend!' She then compares her felicity to that of Blesilla, the daughter of Paula (it is difficult to recognize the Lady Frances in this guise), who was instructed by St Jerome, and to Mammaea, mother of the Emperor Severus, 'all which persons were celebrated for the glory and happiness they derived from the instructions of wise men'. She has read Bullinger's treatise, *Of Christian Perfection* (her noble father would have written about it, but for his weighty engagements), and from it, 'I gather daily, as from a most beautiful garden, the sweetest flowers'. She was gratified by Bullinger's 'commendation of myself, which, as I cannot claim, so I ought not to allow', but would he continue to write to her and to pray for her – 'girlish and unlearned as I am?' She concludes: 'Farewell, brightest ornament and support of the whole Church of Christ, your piety's most devoted Joanna Graia.'[7]

In her next letters Jane complains of the slowness of the couriers – Bradgate is inconveniently remote – and desires advice on the study of Hebrew, so that she may read the Old Testament in the original. 'In writing to you in this manner I have shown more boldness than prudence ... my mind is fluctuating and undecided ... but I write because I desire to learn ... I have acquired but little learning.' She adds cautiously: 'As I acknowledge faith to be God's gift, I ought therefore only to promise religious devotion as He may see fit to bestow it.'[8]

Meanwhile Haddon and Aylmer were writing in a more practical strain. Of course their pupil was a truly marvellous young lady, and they hoped to be able to confirm the reports of her marriage – 'O! if that event should take place, how happy would be the union, and how beneficial to the church!' – but there was some difficulty about the Hebrew studies (perhaps Bullinger had better dedicate to her his translation of the Talmud) and they felt that my Lord Marquess was losing his enthusiasm for the propagation of the true faith. What was to be done? He remained 'a shining light', but he was always too busy to write, or even to glance at the flood of pamphlets and letters their friends poured into Bradgate. (He had, however, increased Bullinger's pension.) Then comes the first critical note in the correspondence. Aylmer, thanking Bullinger for keeping their patron up to the mark, added that the Lady Jane had also benefited, 'for, at that age, *all are inclined to follow their own ways*'. She was like his own daughter, in fact – but – 'to these tender minds there should neither be wanting the counsel of the aged nor the authority of men of grave and influential character'. He concludes with a comment on the improvement in his pupil, which, after his previous high-flown eulogies, sounds a little ominous.[9] To this may be joined Lady Jane's remark about Bullinger's counsels as being especially suited 'to my age, sex, *and the dignity of my family*'.[10] No intellectual humility could make her forget who she was, or what she might become; on that point at least, she and the Dorsets were allied.

Yet even when she was composing an elaborate compliment, some hint of her parents' treatment seems to underlie the cumbersome phrases. 'Were I to extol you as truth requires, I should need either the oratorical powers of Demosthenes or the eloquence of Cicero ... but I am too young and ignorant for either ... In this earthly prison you pass your days as if you were dead, whereas you live, and this not only to Christ in the first place, but also to others without number.'[11] It was not Bullinger who suffered in captivity; he was busy and successful. In reply he sent her his treatise on marriage, which she translated from Latin into Greek. This evoked a paean from Haddon. 'I do not think,' he wrote, 'that among all the English nobility for many ages past there has arisen a single individual who, to the highest excellencies of talent and judgement has

united so much diligence and assiduity to the cultivation of
every liberal pursuit,' adding that Lady Jane's music and
needlework were of as high a standard as her scholarship. In
her turn, Jane planned to send Bullinger's wife a pair of gloves
and a gold ring; at the last moment the ring was withdrawn,
perhaps at the Dorsets' command.[12] She remained steadfast,
and would have asked for nothing better than to study and
write letters in peace. 'Whatever she has begun,' Haddon remarked, 'she will complete — unless she be diverted by some
calamity.'[13] In this, the third year of the Zürich Letters, the
calamities were not far off; very soon Jane was to leave Bradgate for ever.

Meanwhile the disputes about gambling had caused an uproar. After some discussion, the Dorsets yielded to the point of
forbidding their servants to play, while continuing to do so
themselves in their private apartments. To Haddon's protests
the Marquess replied that although he personally did not care
whether he won or lost, the game was unendurably dull without
stakes, and also that he must yield to fashion in this matter. 'Let
the game be cold and lifeless,' urged the chaplain, and proceeded to give his patron a long lecture on his extravagance in
dress ('the fault consists in their being over-abundant') and the
laws against gambling. Dorset evaded both issues, and continued to play. Haddon then announced that if his employer did
not forbear, he would be forced to rebuke him publicly, in his
Christmas sermon. He did so, partly because the Dorsets'
obstinacy was made more odious in his eyes by their allowing
their tenants to keep up the papistical, not to say the pagan,
rites of the season. 'They fancy,' he explained to Bullinger,
'that they are merry after this fashion on account of the birth of
Our Lord. This still prevails among the vulgar ... In our
[household] there is nothing of this kind.'[14]

The Dorsets were so annoyed by Haddon's interference with
their pleasures that he had to give in. 'They are advancing into
what is really evil,' he told Bullinger. 'I bear with this out of
compulsion ... and deal tenderly with them.'[15]

With this part of the correspondence, so uncharacteristic of
the spirit of humanism, Lady Jane's tragedy begins. She was —

perhaps she always had been – of the stuff of which the Puritan martyr is made : self-examining, fanatical, bitterly courageous, and utterly incapable of the art of compromise in which the Tudors specialized. Even Mary, before her judgement became clouded by misery and disease, showed that she knew something of it; Edward, equally fervent, yielded to pressure on more than one occasion. Henry VII and Henry VIII were highly gifted in that respect; and Elizabeth's superb genius shone out in this as in all her other activities. Yet Jane, intellectually the most brilliant of an extraordinary dynasty, never developed the kind of sensitivity to the feelings of others which leads to a change of front. This disability was enhanced, if it had not been actually created, by the combination of her parents' dislike and her tutors' adulation. Alternately abused and toadied, caring only for the things of the mind, she developed a capacity for self-isolation highly uncharacteristic of her day, with the merciless intolerance which was its most unpleasant expression. Just as she would have gone to the stake for her beliefs, so she would have sent anyone else there, when persuasion failed.

She seems, on such slight evidence as exists, to have been fond of Katharine and to have had no affection at all for the hunchbacked Mary. By the time her days of study were over, and she was forced to re-enter the world in which she had already failed, she was guided by a single ideal – the triumph of Protestantism over the old faith – and aware of one political factor, that she might one day become Queen of England. She was a Tudor first, a Grey afterwards, and a Protestant all the time.

NOTES

1. Ascham, *The Schoolmaster* (Everyman edition), p 35.
2. Parker Society, *Original Letters*, vol I, pp 286–7.
3. Elyot, *The Governor*, p 21.
4. Strype, *Life of Aylmer*, p 194.
5. Ibid, p 4.
6. Parker Society, *Original Letters*, vol I, pp 2–11.
7. Ibid, pp 2–275.

8. Ibid.
9. Ibid, pp 272–82, 421–52.
10. Ibid.
11. Ibid, pp 280–2.
12. Ibid, pp 427–33.
13. Ibid.
14. Ibid, pp 454–684.
15. Ibid.

Part II

The Years of Endurance

> Troubled on every side, yet not distressed ... perplexed, but not in despair; persecuted, but not forsaken: cast down, but not destroyed.
>
> *2 Corinthians* iv. 8–9

Chapter 1

The Political Scene

IN October 1551 Lady Jane celebrated her fourteenth birthday. She was now grown up; if her marriage had taken place as originally planned, she would have been leaving home for a household of her own. But the schemes for her future were at a standstill; and she reached maturity in seclusion, far removed from the political scene and the personages who were to control her destiny.

While Jane was studying and composing at Bradgate, the statesmen revolving round Edward VI began to transfer their services from one minister to another. These men, most of them middle-aged, were all unscrupulous, corrupt, and efficient only while their own interests were concerned. The four Councillors with whom Jane and her parents were to have most to do were William Paulet, Marquess of Winchester, Treasurer and Lord Chancellor; Henry Fitzalan, Earl of Arundel, Chamberlain to the King; the Earl of Pembroke; and William Parr, Marquess of Northampton and Great Chamberlain of England. Winchester, who was to outlive all the others, having served four out of the five Tudor monarchs, described himself as rather of the nature of the willow than of the oak; Arundel was crudely self-seeking and treacherous; Pembroke specialized in sycophancy; and Northampton, outwardly unremarkable, was quietly set on his own advancement and power.

These men, declared converts to the reformed faith, lived without God, although, like everyone else in their world, they observed the usual rites and were regular churchgoers. They were now uniting behind the subtlest, the most brilliant and the most evil of all the English statesmen in the sixteenth century: John Dudley, Duke of Northumberland, who was already considering an alliance between Lady Jane and his fifth and only

unmarried son, Lord Guilford Dudley. The fact that the
Dorsets had promised Jane to Somerset's eldest boy, who came
to their London house and was on intimate terms with them,
did not matter to Northumberland, for he had arrived at the
point when he was about to destroy, not only Somerset's power,
but the man himself.

Northumberland had reached this, his penultimate objective,
after more than twenty years of steady progress as soldier,
sailor and politician. As is so often the case with men of his
type, he began life under a cloud. He was the eldest son of
Henry VII's chief minister, Edmund Dudley, whom Henry
VIII executed, with his fellow-lawyer and associate, Empson,
as soon as he came to the throne. John Dudley's origins were
noble; his paternal grandfather was a Knight of the Garter and
Steward to Henry V; his mother, Elizabeth de Lisle, was a
descendant of Warwick the King-Maker.

John was born in 1501. After his father's execution in 1509
he was adopted by Sir Richard Guilford, whose daughter he
married in 1520. In the course of the next twenty years he
became Lord High Admiral, Master of the Horse, Viscount
Lisle and the father of thirteen children, seven of whom sur-
vived to follow his fortunes. A first-class athlete (he was the
finest jouster of his day), an elegant, handsome and accomplished courtier and a skilled administrator, he remained one of
the King's most valued servants. When Henry VIII died and
Somerset was made Protector, Dudley showed his adaptability
by relinquishing the Admiraltyship to Thomas Seymour in ex-
change for the earldom of Warwick and a place on the Council
board, without complaint; but he resented Somerset's forcing
him to do so.

He therefore began to undermine Somerset's authority by
blackguarding him to the French envoys, who came to pay
Henri II's respects to Edward VI on his accession. Dudley
visited them privately, expressed his horror of the reformed
religion – which he had embraced ten years before – and added,
'Out of twelve who kneel seven would willingly cut the throats
of both the King and the Duke of Somerset. The Duke and the
Lord Admiral have made themselves impregnable,' he went on

in his fluent French, 'we must needs wait for a *coup de main*, from God. But within these three years we shall see an end of their greatness.'[1]

'*Nous le prenions pour fort habile homme*,' said the French secretary, when Thomas Seymour was executed in 1549, Somerset lost the Protectorship in 1550, and it became plain that the downfall of both brothers had been partially and secretly engineered by Dudley. In 1549 he achieved his greatest triumph by his victory over the Norfolk rebels in their attempt to destroy the enclosure system. He was much praised, not only for his skill and courage, but for his mercy towards the prisoners. When his small force was threatened with extinction, he drew his sword, kissed the blade and spoke of death before dishonour. When the campaign was over, he replied to his officers' appeals for revenge with more practical rhetoric. 'Is there no place for pardon?' he demanded. 'What shall we then do? Shall we hold the plough ourselves, play the carters and labour the ground with our own hands?'[2]

Between the summer of 1550 and the autumn of 1551 Northumberland reorganized the Regency Council of which Somerset had been the head, on what appeared to be an equal basis. He worked so unobtrusively that not even his closest associates – and certainly not Somerset, whose daughter Anne had just married his eldest son – perceived the extent of his power. His primary object was the subjugation of the King, whom he fascinated and impressed by his skill at games – he always, somehow, made time to shoot with Edward at the butts – by his fervent Protestantism and, most important of all, by his stressing of the royal prerogative. Northumberland treated the conscientious, high-minded, enthusiastic boy as if he had already attained his majority. While advising, he deferred to and consulted Edward in private, and insisted on his presence at Council meetings.[3]

Having prepared the ground and bribed a number of climbers and hangers-on to bear false witness against Somerset, it was an easy matter to bring a charge of high treason against the Duke, who in November 1551 was accused of plotting to murder the Council and reinstate his own dictatorship. Dudley

and twenty-six of his peers, sitting in judgement at Westminster Hall, condemned their former leader on four out of five
counts. Dudley took the opportunity to harangue his old com-
rade in solemn commiseration. 'O! Duke of Somerset,' he
began, 'you see yourself brought into the utmost danger, and
that nothing but death awaits you. I have once before delivered
you from a similar hazard of your life [he was referring to
Somerset's disgrace and imprisonment in 1550], and I will
not now desist from serving you ... As for myself, I shall willingly forgive you everything, and will use every exertion in my
power that your life may be spared.'[4]

After he had thus drawn attention to his own generosity of
spirit and shown that he alone had the power to obtain Somerset's pardon, Northumberland had to play his cards very carefully. The people's love for Somerset and Edward's reluctance
to destroy him made immediate execution impossible; he must
remain in the Tower till the excitement caused by his trial had
died down. He did not reach the scaffold till January 1552, and
there, after a disturbance which very nearly ended in his being
rescued by the mob, died asseverating his loyalty to his nephew.
Meanwhile Arundel, who had been involved in Somerset's
downfall, was imprisoned for a year and heavily fined; he came
out of the Tower determined to revenge himself on Northumberland, who by this time had achieved his own dukedom. Both
King and Council were now united behind Northumberland,
while chafing against his power.

Northumberland's private life was impeccable. He neither
drank nor gamed; his wife and children were loyal and co-
operative, and no disputes took place within his splendid,
bustling household, even when its head was living under the
combined pressure of anxiety, overwork and poor health. In
fact, Northumberland had always trained his family to work
together for their common interests. Yet his attitude towards
them was rather business-like than affectionate, as is shown in
a letter to William Cecil (now knighted and his secretary)
announcing the death of his seven-year-old daughter Tem-
perance. Northumberland's chief concern was to explain that,
in the event of her having had some infectious disease, he would

be unable to appear at Court till he was out of quarantine; he therefore described the child's symptoms and the state of her corpse ('between the shoulders it was very black') without a sign of feeling, and this to one of his most intimate associates – for he had no friends. While allowing for the detachment then felt by the majority of parents about their children, we may yet perceive in this letter the icy heartlessness which was one of the writer's most formidable weapons.[5]

It was part of Northumberland's policy to give both sons and daughters a first-class education, equal to that provided for the Tudors and the Greys. (The boys' tutor was Dr John Dee, the geographer and mathematician, who was trained at the Universities of Louvain and Paris and became famous under Queen Elizabeth.[6]) The male Dudleys were brought up on the Elyot–Ascham principle, not only as scholars, linguists, athletes and musicians, but as future statesmen and administrators. The great Duke's dark-eyed, ruthless brood were perfectly disciplined; they never rebelled against their father and remained faithful to him when disaster overtook them all.

The secret of his power lay partly in the charm he was able to exercise over almost everyone he met. Two people disliked and feared him from the beginning to the end of their relationship: the Princess Mary and Lady Jane. In Mary's case, there was good reason, for she and Northumberland were natural enemies; yet even when he stood at the head of the State (although he refused all official positions) as the 'thunderbolt and terror of the Papists' and the King's right hand, Jane appears to have hated him. She shrank indeed from all the Dudleys: but then she was not a girl who took to people easily. As far as young men were concerned, her heart remained inviolate. In the first months of their acquaintance, Guilford's polished address and handsome face made no impression; and as time went on, she saw him for what he was – an over-indulged, conceited, silly youth.

There were a number of others who, if they had ever come into contact with her, would have agreed with Lady Jane about Northumberland. The common people, who remembered Somerset as their 'good Duke' and Protector, detested his destroyer and continued to believe in his innocence. (And even if His Grace had planned to murder Northumberland and the others – why not? Were they not all villains?) From the moment of Somerset's arrest many of the country folk had guessed at Northumberland's darker purposes. Thomas Holland of Bath, visiting his relations in the capital, showed them one of the new shillings; there were the Warwick-Dudley emblems, the bear and ragged staff. ' 'Tis no more than a lion's head,' said the Londoner. 'Tush, tush, hold thy peace, fool!' replied Holland in his rustic drawl. 'Thou shalt see another world ere Candlemass. The Duke of Somerset shall go forth from the Tower, and the Duke of Northumberland shall go in.'[7]

Two years later that prophecy was realized, although not quite as the speaker intended. Somerset had come out of the Tower to the scaffold, and his great enemy had entered it by Traitors' Gate. Northumberland's most fatal mistake was that he never considered the people and completely discounted the personality of Lady Jane. This negligence made his ruin inevitable.

ii

In July 1551 Frances Dorset's two half-brothers died of the sweating sickness and she and her husband became Duke and Duchess of Suffolk. They then took up permanent positions at Court and occupied a suite of rooms at Richmond Palace. Here the Duchess fell ill and sent for Lady Jane to help nurse her. As soon as she recovered, all three came to London in order to receive Mary of Guise, the Queen Regent of Scotland, who was being entertained by Edward and his ministers. So Jane made her second public appearance loaded with jewels and gorgeously dressed – against her will, it would seem, for she was now involved in a controversy about fashion which had driven the Tudor family into opposite camps.

Latimer, the most popular and also the most ultra-Protestant preacher, constantly inveighed against the extravagance and ostentation of the nobles in his sermons at Whitehall. Edward, delighting in finery, continued to appear in gold tissue, violet silk and white velvet glittering with emeralds, rubies and diamonds.[8] Mary followed his example. Elizabeth adopted the new, plain style of dress – and so did Lady Jane, partly because Aylmer urged it and partly, it may be, because her parents covered themselves with gewgaws at every opportunity. And in her mind, the fact that the Popish Lady Mary followed the old fashion was another reason for adopting the simpler 'puritan' modes.

Mary, generous, affectionate and extravagant, loved to give presents – very often they cost more than she could afford[9] – and just before Jane left Bradgate to receive the Scottish Queen, sent her some 'goodly apparel of tinsel cloth of gold and velvet, laid on with parchment lace of gold'. When the parcel was undone, Jane contemplated the shining folds in silence. Then she said, 'What shall I do with it?' Her old nurse, Mrs Ellen, said briskly, 'Marry, wear it, to be sure,' 'Nay,' Jane replied, 'that were a shame to follow my Lady Mary against God's word, and leave my Lady Elizabeth which followeth God's word' – to the delight of Aylmer, who described the scene in a letter to Ascham.[10] Next Christmas, which she and her parents spent with the elder Princess, Jane so far forgot her principles as to accept Mary's gift of a pearl and ruby necklace. The red drops were drawn closely round her throat, in the fashion of the time . . .[11]

In dress, as in other matters, Jane was overborne when she attended the festivities organized for the reception of the Queen Regent. Northumberland, in his fifty-second year and still one of the best-looking men of his day, was another splendid figure. He and his sons – John, now Earl of Warwick, Henry, Ambrose, Guilford, and Robert, the tallest and handsomest of them all, who had recently married Amy Robsart – had brilliant good looks and bore themselves with superb hauteur. Indeed, it seems as if this family put everyone else in the shade. Mary Dudley, the wife of Henry Sidney, Edward's cup-bearer and one of his greatest friends, was then at her best. (A few years later she was completely disfigured by smallpox.) Guilford, fair-haired, graceful and elegant, was his mother's favourite, and she was allowed to spoil him; he appealed to her when he could not get what he wanted. 'Of all Dudley's brood,' says a seventeenth-century historian, 'he had nothing of the father in him.'[12] It may have been so; certainly the sixteen-year-old Guilford had neither the Duke's brains nor the Duchess' force of character. He thought very well of himself nevertheless, was rabidly ambitious and would have liked to emulate his father, whose domination of the Government was to last two more years.

No one studying his manoeuvres between January 1552 and March 1553 could have guessed that Northumberland would lose the territory he had gained. This consisted in his command of the King, absolute control of the State and the maintenance of England as an international power, holding the balance between the great empires of France and Spain. Northumberland's technique is best described by Sir Richard Morrison. 'This earl', he said, 'had such a head that he seldom went about anything but he had three or four purposes beforehand.'[13]

Northumberland's plans for the marriage of Jane and Guilford were still fluid, partly because he was considering what might be a more profitable union. The alternative to Lady Jane was her first cousin, Lady Margaret Clifford, the daughter of Frances Suffolk's younger sister Eleanor, the late Countess of Cumberland. Lady Margaret's claim to the throne was remote; but Northumberland had the King's approval of the marriage, and it was still in his mind.[14] Finally he arranged an alliance between his brother, Sir Andrew Dudley, and the Cumberland heiress; at the last moment Lady Margaret's father refused to coöperate, and the match fell through.

Northumberland now had to concentrate on a very grave problem indeed – that of the King's health. Edward had not always been the sickly boy described by so many historians. Apart from a bout of malaria in 1542, from which he completely recovered, he did not have a single serious illness and led an active, outdoor life (his diary abounds in accounts of hunting, archery contests and running at the ring[15]) till the April of 1552, when he succumbed to an attack of measles; this sowed the seeds of the tuberculosis of which he died sixteen months later. Some time in the spring of the following year, it became plain to Northumberland that Edward would not live to attain his majority, and that in order to maintain his own power, he would have to reconstitute the arrangements for the succession. He began by placing the French marriage in the background, while declaring himself 'wholly French' to the resident Ambassador, and made plans for depriving the Princess Mary of her right to the crown. In the event of his being able to do so – her Catholicism would be the basis of this project – there yet remained the Princess Elizabeth, whose adherence to the reformed faith was fervent and carefully advertised. Both Princesses were very popular, Mary possibly a little more so than Elizabeth.

With regard to Elizabeth, Northumberland's machinations were brief and obscure. At one time he considered marrying her to Guilford.[16] Then it became clear that it would be impossible to manipulate this extremely clever young lady: in no way would she fit into his schemes; and although she behaved correctly, he had the feeling that she did not like him. He therefore set about estranging her from the King, keeping her away from Court and stressing, whenever possible, that although Henry VIII had placed her next in the succession to Mary, she was still technically illegitimate.[17]

Thus, if the elimination of the Princesses materialized and Edward died within the next four years, Frances Suffolk was the rightful Queen. (Mary Stuart, as Queen Regnant of one foreign country and resident in another, did not count, apart from the fact that she had been cut out of Henry's will.) This would not do at all. Northumberland knew very well that, although he might do what he liked with Suffolk, his wife was quite unmanageable. She would destroy the power of the Dudleys without hesitation. The obvious tactics were to ally her interests with his by marrying Jane to Guilford and persuading or bribing Frances to relinquish her claim to the succession to her daughter. It was a pity that Guilford was neither the heir nor up to his brothers' standards; and for a short time Northumberland contemplated divorcing John Dudley from his wife Anne Seymour in order to give him to Jane.[18]

(These matters could always be arranged.) He then reverted to his first plan of marrying Guilford to Jane, with the proviso that Frances Suffolk would make way for her if Edward died.

All these considerations depended on Edward VI. As the boy developed and began to enforce his own decisions (it had been difficult enough to get him to sign Somerset's death-warrant [19]) Northumberland became very anxious. If Edward regained his health and married Elisabeth of France, to whom he was now contracted, how would the Dudleys stand? Meanwhile, the Duke continued to play off France against Spain and the moderates against the ultra-Protestants (Bishop Hooper went too far and Cranmer not far enough), to keep on outwardly good terms with the Princesses and the more influential members of the Council and, of course, to flatter the Suffolks, who were beginning to mistrust him. Northumberland's correspondence shows his day to have been a full one. He visited the King secretly, at night, taking care never to advise him in the presence of others.[20] The result was that he began to live on his nerves, and could not always sustain the informal geniality which came as a pleasant surprise to those meeting him for the first time.

Northumberland was a better and more natural actor than most politicians; but now his jokes had a cutting edge, and his outbursts of temper were more frequent. The detailed and almost daily reports of de Scheyve, the Spanish Ambassador, who spent many hours alone with him, show a loss of control of which Northumberland himself was not at first aware. Then, as if he realized how terrifying his rages were and how much more quickly they forced his will on his opponents, he seems to have indulged in them deliberately. The process is clearly seen in the half-admiring, half-suspicious descriptions of the envoy, whose duty it was to break up the French alliance. (It was better His Majesty should marry the Protestant Lady Jane than Elisabeth of France.) The great Duke reassured de Scheyve. Old friends were best, he said; he knew very well how treacherous the French were: Spanish support would never fail. As for Protestantism – there was no need for His Most Christian Majesty's alarm. The English people were really Catholic – and therefore pro-Spanish – at heart.[21] Then Northumberland would shut himself up to write letters which not even the ubiquitous and indispensable Cecil was allowed to see, going to bed, as he told the secretary, 'with a careful heart and a weary body'.[22]

The Suffolks, on the other hand, were tireless. With Lady Jane and a vast following they continued to make the rounds, visiting the King while he was on progress at Oxford and staying at the houses of relations and friends. In the October of 1550 they stayed with the Willoughbys at Tilty in Essex for two months 'with all their train'. Dinner-parties were given for the neighbours, the most important being the Princess Mary, then in her thirty-fourth year. They were entertained by a party of strolling players and also by Lord Oxford's private company. Then they all went on to the Audleys, near by, returning to Tilty for more dinner-parties.[23]

As a result of all these late nights and journeyings, Lady Jane fell ill. As soon as she recovered she and her parents went to stay with Princess Mary at Newhall in Essex. There, in spite of the Council's objections, Edward's personal veto, Northumberland's browbeating and the fact that she was breaking the law, the Princess Mary's Mass was celebrated daily, and the Host stood on the altar. Jane restrained all outward expressions of horror and disgust, until, passing through the chapel with Lady Anne Wharton, she stopped as she saw the gentlewoman curtsy.

'Why do you so? Is the Lady Mary in the chapel?' she rather disingenuously inquired. 'No, Madam,' said the other girl, 'I make my curtsy to Him that made us all.' The Protestant slogans – 'Beware of familiarity of Papists – beware of unhonest practices [24] – sounded like trumpet-calls. 'Why,' said Lady Jane, 'how can He be there that made us all, and the baker made Him?' This remark was immediately repeated to the Princess.

Mary had been very fond of her little cousin. Now she recoiled. 'Thereafter,' gleefully records a Protestant contemporary, 'the Lady Mary did never love the Lady Jane, but esteemed her as the rest of that Christian profession.' [25]

NOTES

1. Chapman, *The Last Tudor King*, p 102.

2. Holinshed, *Chronicle*, vol III, p 981.

3. Chapman, p 210.

4. *Literary Remains of Edward VI*, vol II, p 374; *Original Letters*, ser 2, p 441; Cobbett, *State Trials*, vol I, pp 483–506.

5. Tytler, *England under the Reigns of Edward VI and Mary*, vol II, p 114.

6. Williamson, *The Tudor Age*, p 216.

7. Chapman, p 232.

8. Ibid, p 218.

9. Madden, *Expenses of Princess Mary*, p 85.

10. Strype, *Life of Aylmer*, pp 195–6.

11. Madden, p 85.

12. Heylyn, *History of the Reformation*, p 150.

13. Nichols, *Literary Remains of Edward VI*, vol II, p clxv.

14. Strickland, *Lives of the Tudor and Stuart Princesses*, p 187.

15. Chapman, p 218.

16. *Cal SP Spanish*, vol XI, p 38.

17. Ibid.

18. Ibid.

19. Chapman, p 232.

20. Ibid, p 211.

21. *Cal SP Spanish*, vol XI, p 17.

22. Tytler, p 161.

23. Middleton MSS, pp 519–21.

24. Harington, *Nugae Antiquae*, vol II, p 187.

25. Holinshed, vol IV, p 2311.

Chapter 2

The Marriage of Lady Jane

A C C O R D I N G to modern standards, Lady Jane's behaviour to the Princess Mary was bigoted, pert and fanatical. In her own day, and for at least a hundred and fifty years after it, her remarks about the Host and about Mary's present of a dress were quoted as proofs of her high principles and clearness of mind. Contemporary Protestants considered that she was right not only in her opinions, but in so expressing them, no matter how blasphemous they might seem to those of the opposite persuasion.

In their arguments about the Eucharist both Catholics and Protestants admitted two constituent elements in the bread and wine – the 'accidents' and the 'substance' of each. By 'accidents' they meant the shape, colour and weight, as perceived by the senses: by 'substance', the deepest underlying reality, not taken in by any of the senses, but assumed by the reason to exist. The Catholics believed that at the moment of consecration the accidents of the bread and wine remained unaltered, while the substance of the bread changed into the substance of the true living Body of Christ, and the substance of the wine into the substance of His Blood. The extreme Protestant view (rejected by the Henricians, or Anglo-Catholics) was that it could not be proved from Scripture that Christ's Body and Blood were actually present in the substance of the bread and wine. His Presence could only be received by faith; therefore the rite was at the same time a pledge through which the communicant's redemption was renewed and a memorial to the Redeemer.

The controversy about transubstantiation was one for which many persons were ready to die – and did die – in terrible agony. Courtesy and self-restraint could have no place in an arena where life and death, and eternal damnation or the reverse were at stake. The person despised and condemned was one who remained silent when given the chance, as Lady Jane was given it on these and other occasions, to bear witness for the faith.

Also, the Real Presence in the sacrament was the most popular, because the most dangerous, topic of the day, one for which anyone of any mental capacity at all was prepared to give battle for hours at a time. It provided thrilling intellectual contests and highly enjoyable arguments for a people whose principal reading was theological. (About seventy-five per cent of the books published before 1550 were sermons or religious treatises). A typical instance of this pursuit is provided by Edward Underhill, the Protestant 'Hot Gospeller', whose career touched that of Lady Jane just before her death, and whose fragmentary reminiscences re-create a section of her world. When he was stationed at Calais as Master of the Ordinance to the Earl of Huntingdon (who also was to be connected with the fortunes of the Suffolk family), Underhill was often 'set on' by Huntingdon to amuse him at the expense of his brother, Sir Edward Hastings. 'The Earl being vested with sickness,' says Underhill, '... for that I could sing and play to the lute, would have me with him in his chamber, and had also a great delight to hear his brother reason with me in matters of religion, who would be very hot when I did overlay him with texts of the Scripture, concerning the natural presence of Christ in the sacrament of the altar, and would swear great oaths – especially "by the Lord's foot" – that, after the words spoken by the priest, there remained no bread, but the natural body that Mary bare. "Nay, then, it must needs be," would I say, "if you prove it with such oaths." Whereas the said Earl would laugh heartily, saying "Brother, give him over, Underhill is too good for you." Wherewith [Hastings] would be very angry.'[1]

In fact, no educated and religious person worthy of the name would have ignored the challenge presented to Lady Jane in the chapel at Newhall. And the more forcibly – according to present-day rules, the more offensively – she replied to it, the better her response. To visualize that scene as her contemporaries did is to lift the veil which divides one age from another.

So it was that in the sixteenth century the ultra-Protestant attitude towards belief in the Real Presence became one of shuddering repulsion. To assert that a miracle had been performed which enabled the communicant to feed on the substance of the Body and Blood of Jesus Christ turned the service – so persons of Lady Jane's persuasion declared – into a cannibal act, a desecration of the most sacred of all rites. 'Wilt thou,' she wrote a year later, 'torment again, rend and tear the most precious Body of our Saviour Christ with thy bodily and fleshly teeth?'[2] Her cousin Edward's rhyme summed up this view.

> Not with our teeth His flesh to tear,
> Nor take blood for our drink;
> Too great absurdity it were
> So grossly for to think.[3]

The human Body of the Redeemer, so she and her party asseverated, 'was ascended into Heaven and placed on the right hand of God the Father; therefore it could not be situate upon earth in the sacrament of the altar.'[4] It was the custom in both Protestant and Catholic circles to reinforce their arguments on this point with patristic quotations, and Basil the Great was one of their common authorities. In the Christmas week of 1552 an unnamed lady sent Lady Jane a book of selections from this bishop's works with a letter in Greek describing its contents as 'more valuable than gold or precious stones'. 'Its perusal,' she added, 'will raise the soul, grovelling and set on earthly things, to God the Almighty.'[5]

To those Protestants occupied in raising their souls, every opportunity to demonstrate against all manifestations of the Catholic God – whom Lady Jane described as 'a detestable idol, invented by Romish Popes and the abominable college of crafty cardinals'[6] – brought them one step nearer eternal happiness. When she wrote 'Labour always to learn to die'[7] she was not reiterating a slogan, or even a thought; she was expressing the inspiration of her daily conduct. She lived in the presence of God, and thus under His sentence of death, long before she received that of her cousin Mary – by which time she had learnt the lesson perfectly.

In 1552 Lady Jane's beliefs were enforced on the nation by the publication of the Second Prayer Book of Edward VI which, later rejected for that of 1549, clarified and emphasized the Protestant denial of transubstantiation, and coincided with the substitution of tables for altars. That these innovations shocked and distressed the majority of the English people did not concern Lady Jane, for her temperament and education had combined to isolate her socially. She remained unaware of what those outside her immediate circle were thinking and wanting, while Edward, Mary and Elizabeth were all, in different degrees, in touch with them, just as their father had been. Except for Aylmer and her correspondents in Switzerland, Jane stood alone, partly perhaps, because she preferred to be so. In this, her sixteenth year, neither her languages nor her reading had brought her into contact with the world of every day. Now the time had come for her to enter it, through her parents' and Northumberland's manoeuvres – for they were finally agreed on their plan of action.

ii

Edward VI recovered from his attack of measles (wrongly diagnosed as smallpox) by the end of April 1552. During the spring and summer of that year he appeared to be in excellent health and spirits and was carrying out all his duties as usual.[8] In July he set off on progress, returning to Windsor on September 15th. It then became clear that he was not only over-exhausted but beginning to show symptoms of serious illness. The celebrated Milanese doctor, Cardano, was called in and made a private diagnosis of consumption. 'I saw,' he said afterwards, 'the omens of a great calamity.' He dared not give his opinion to the Privy Council, partly because, not having been allowed to examine Edward, he could not be sure how ill he really was, and partly because to hint at his death might result in a charge of high treason. All he could do was to prescribe a less strenuous routine for His Majesty and leave him to the mercies of the Court physicians.[9]

Between October 1552 and January 1553 Edward's condition steadily deteriorated. On January 20th de Scheyve reported that a crisis was coming. Northumberland was amassing great sums of money, and had taken over the finances of the kingdom from Winchester. On February 21st he called a new Parliament and Edward, now fifteen, was given his majority three years before it was due. By this time Northumberland was so sure of his hold over the boy that he could count on exercising absolute power from behind the screen of the royal prerogative. He was dictator of England, and hated accordingly – except by the dying King, who had begun to suspect his own condition and placed his whole trust in the Duke. Edward believed that Northumberland was as dedicated as he himself to the Protestant cause, the reformation of the currency and the plans for foreign trade and exploration on which he had spent so many hours, filling page after page with analyses and sub-headings in his schoolboy scrawl. Now, too weary to continue, he secretly handed everything over to Northumberland, while continuing to fight his disease and insist that he was only temporarily disabled.[10] By the middle of March the Duke had decided on his immediate actions and was beginning to cover his tracks.

The first thing to do was to conceal his control of affairs and to provide against emergencies by treating the Princess Mary as heiress presumptive – for it was still assumed that Edward and Elisabeth of France would marry and continue the dynasty. He therefore wrote to Mary about the King's health, arranged for her to visit him and, through de Scheyve, made it clear that his only desire was to serve her and his country; he had no ambitions for himself.[11] To Cecil he wrote resignedly and plaintively ('scribbled in my bed as ill at ease as I have been all my life') that he resembled the faithful servant in the Italian proverb, who became 'a perpetual ass'. If only he had his health – but he was old and sick. 'What comfort think you may I have, that seeth myself in this case after my long travail

and troublesome life, and towards the end of my days? ...
What should I want any longer this life? ... I have no great
cause to tarry much longer here.'[12]

This mood of Christian meekness lasted till the second week
in April when, at a session of both Houses, Cranmer read out
his suggestions for the reform of canon law. Northumberland,
realizing that these might impinge on his authority, started up
in one of his terrifying rages. 'You bishops!' he shouted, 'look
to it at your peril that you touch not the doings of your peers!
Take heed that the like happen not again – or you and your
preachers shall suffer for it together!' Cranmer, the mildest of
men, protested. The clergy, he said, had spoken of 'vices and
abuses', that was all. 'There are vices enough!' exclaimed the
Duke, 'make no doubt of that!' He added with strange frankness, 'The fruits of the Gospel are meagre enough.' He then
warned the House that to alter the laws might resuscitate
Popery, and reminded them of the King's determination to
enforce the reformed faith.[13]

A week later Northumberland, convinced that Edward's
days were numbered, announced the betrothal of Lady Jane
Grey and Lord Guilford Dudley. On the same day, or shortly
before it, the Suffolks, now in their London house, summoned
Jane and told her what had been decided. An extraordinary
scene ensued.

A hundred years later it was not unknown for girls to reject
their parents' choice of a husband; and records exist of tears
and protests being made which sometimes ended in point-blank
refusals to obey. In the sixteenth century such an attitude was
virtually unheard of – except in the case of Lady Jane's grandmother, Mary Tudor, who, when told that she was to marry
Louis XII, cried, stormed and only gave in after making Henry
VIII promise that her next husband should be selected by herself. The fifteen-year-old Lady Jane neither wept nor
pleaded. She simply said that she would not marry Guilford
Dudley.*

* Raviglio Rosso, *Historia delle cose occorse nel regno d'Inghilterra*,
p 8. There are three contemporary Italian sources for Lady Jane's own
account of her feelings before and after her marriage: Rosso, Pollini

The Suffolks' amazement soon gave way to furious vocifera-
tion. Lady Jane then pointed out that, having already been contracted to Lord Hertford, she was not free to marry anyone else.
No written records of this agreement survive, doubtless because
the Suffolks destroyed them; but it was referred to as official –
and therefore almost as binding as a marriage – not only by
Lady Jane but, later, by Queen Mary.[14]

Their daughter's habit of putting them in the wrong had its
usual effect on the Suffolks, and they resorted to violence. The
Duke swore at her; the Duchess beat her. And thus, according
to a contemporary, 'by blows from the mother and curses from
the father, they succeeded in concluding [the marriage].'[15] By
the time the conflict ended Jane was committed to Guilford
and, presumably, resigned, for in the days that followed she
made no attempt to alter her situation.

Whether she made this stand because she was attracted to
Hertford (an extremely charming and agreeable young man,
whom her sister Katherine married clandestinely nine years
later[16]) or because she disliked Guilford, or because she did not
want to marry anybody at all, will never be known. Thenceforward her attitude towards Guilford was correct but withdrawn. There is some evidence that in their last months of life
he became fond of her; it is unlikely that he had the least feeling for her at the time of their marriage.

The Suffolks' arbitrary treatment of Hertford – who, in
spite of Somerset's attainder and execution, remained at Court
and on intimate terms with Edward VI – did not affect their
relationship. The Duchess still called him 'son', and he continued to visit them.[17] It may be that at about this time he was
first drawn to the thirteen-year-old Katherine Grey, who was
exquisitely pretty: but whatever hopes he had of marrying her
were put an end to by Northumberland's and the Suffolks'

and Florio. The fullest, Pollini's, is a translation of her letter to Queen
Mary, of which the original has disappeared. Froude and Miss Strickland cite 'Baoardo' as their authority for these passages; by this they
mean Badoaro (or Badoer), the Venetian, whom Rosso mentions in his
preface as having read his book and approved of it. Florio's version is
based on Foxe's and Pollini's narratives.

arrangements for further strengthening their position through more profitable alliances.

A few days after the betrothal of Jane and Guilford, Katherine Grey was contracted to Lord Herbert, Pembroke's heir (Pembroke was one of Northumberland's most powerful supporters), and Katherine Dudley was betrothed to Lord Hastings, Huntingdon's eldest son. This youth's maternal grandmother was the Countess of Salisbury, niece of Edward IV, executed by Henry VIII in 1541. The humpbacked Mary Grey, now eight years old, was contracted to a cousin, Lord Arthur Grey, whose father was another adherent of Northumberland.

Thus Northumberland allied himself, through Guilford and Katherine Dudley, with the Tudors and the Plantagenets respectively; and Suffolk, by marrying Katherine Grey to Pembroke's son, was bound to Northumberland's chief ally. It was then decided that the marriages of Jane and Guilford, Katherine Dudley and Hastings, and Katherine Grey and Herbert should be celebrated immediately and simultaneously. Mary Grey was not to be married to Arthur Grey until she reached the age of puberty.

After Pembroke, Huntingdon was, or seemed to be, Northumberland's most valuable supporter. He had been one of Somerset's judges, and was rewarded by a place on the Privy Council. Northumberland did not know that Huntingdon was bitterly jealous of Suffolk and determined to ruin him at the first opportunity. The great Duke trusted no one, least of all Suffolk, Huntingdon and Pembroke; but he believed, and with reason, that their interests were now too closely bound up with his own for them to desert or betray him.

Indeed, his position appeared impregnable. He had absolute control of King, Army, Navy and all departments of State. He had terrorized the clergy, and so manoeuvred the French and Spanish Ambassadors as to make Henri II and Charles V feel themselves dependent on his actions and schemes. Neither potentate dared displease him; and both were ready to sacrifice the Catholic cause in England rather than lose the Duke's support in their struggles against one another.

To weave all these threads into a single, unbreakable strand was a fearful task, and from time to time Northumberland's health gave way under the strain. Yet his care for detail and his grasp of every aspect of the situation never failed. He now possessed three London palaces: Durham House on the Strand, which he seized after Edward VI had promised it to the Princess Elizabeth, Ely Place in Holborn and Sion House in Isleworth, besides the manors of Otford and Penshurst in Kent and suites of rooms at Westminster and Whitehall. As Sion was the largest of these properties, it became his principal residence, and the three marriages should have been celebrated there; but as Northumberland required the invalid King's presence at this event, he decided that it must take place at Durham House. He had begun re-decorating it when Edward's physicians forbade his remaining in the city, and he was removed to Greenwich, never to return alive. Northumberland gave out that His Majesty would come to the weddings, and went on with his purchases and arrangements of tapestries, Turkish carpets and an altar-front sewn with pearls for the chapel, covering walls and furniture in the state rooms with gold and crimson tissue.[18] His brother, Sir Andrew Dudley, whom he summoned back from his embassy in France, was then empowered to choose what he thought best for the six young people from the King's wardrobe; he selected a quantity of jewels, and several lengths of cloth of gold and silver. Neither the Princesses nor the French and Spanish Ambassadors were invited to the triple wedding, which took place on May 25th.[19]

On the morning of that day, Lady Jane was dressed in a gown of gold and silver brocade sewn with diamonds and pearls. Her hair, flowing over her shoulders, was plaited with strings of pearls.[20] Attended by their parents and their ladies, she and Katherine took barge to Durham House, where they were received by the Northumberlands, the Huntingdons, the Warwicks, Pembroke, Winchester and other members of the Council and the Dudley family.

The service was followed by feasting, masques and jousts of royal splendour. A few hours later Guilford Dudley and several of the guests succumbed to food poisoning. Next day the Spanish Ambassador reported their recovery, adding that 'a mistake was made by a Cook, who plucked one leaf for another'.[21]

As soon as the rejoicings, if one may so describe them, were over, Northumberland hurried back to Greenwich, having agreed with Pembroke and the Suffolks that Jane and Katherine should return with their parents to Suffolk Place. Neither marriage was to be consummated as yet; this meant that they could be more easily dissolved if necessary. A few days later Jane resumed her correspondence with Bullinger about her Hebrew studies.

NOTES

1. *Narratives of the Reformation*, ed Nichols, pp 136–8.
2. Foxe, *Acts and Monuments*, vol VI, p 419.
3. *Literary Remains of Edward VI*, ed Nichols, vol I, p 206.
4. Foxe, vol VI, p 408.
5. *Cal SP Domestic*, vol XIV, p 39.
6. Foxe, vol VI, p 419.
7. Ibid.
8. Chapman, *The Last Tudor King*, pp 250–1.
9. Ibid, p 268.
10. *Cal SP Spanish*, vol XI, p 17.
11. Tytler, *England under the Reigns of Edward VI and Mary*, vol II, p 155.
12. Chapman, p 270; *Cal SP Spanish*, vol XI, p 33.
13. Ibid, p 168.
14. Raviglio Rosso, *Historia delle cose occorse nel regno d'Inghilterra*, p 8.
15. Chapman, p 270.
16. Ibid, p 180.
17. Howard, *Life of Lady Jane Grey*, p 194.
18. *Cal SP Spanish*, vol XI, p 53.
19. Howard, p 194.
20. *Cal SP Spanish*, vol XI, p 53.
21. Howard, p 149.

Chapter 3

The Death of Edward VI

THE three marriages celebrated on that Whit Sunday of 1553 sealed Northumberland's immediate possession of England and ensured, so most people believed, his continuity to rule after the death of Edward VI. This last calamity now seemed imminent and was freely spoken of, in spite of the Duke's reassuring bulletins and, a fortnight before the weddings, the pillorying of a man and two women for 'most false and untrue reports touching the King's Majesty's life'.[1]

At the same time, other unnamed persons began to whisper about poison, and to connect Northumberland's remaining by the King's bedside with designs of which he was innocent. In fact, until his plans for Lady Jane's succession had been carried out, the dying boy was the Duke's principal safeguard; yet neither the common people nor the foreign Ambassadors grasped this aspect of the situation. There was young Robert Dudley, for instance, gentleman of the Privy Chamber and carver to His Majesty – surely the King had begun to decline soon after these appointments were made?[2] And was not the magnificence of the wedding festivities intended to cover up Northumberland's wish to destroy his master, who was now concealed from the public – perhaps already dead? It was useless for the Duke to announce that His Majesty was walking in the gardens and galleries of Greenwich; so he told Edward's attendants to hold up the shaking, ghastly figure at a window of the palace in order to show that there was still a king in England. Then everyone knew the worst; and, execrating the very name of Dudley, began fearfully to wonder in what manner and with how much bloodshed Northumberland was going to deprive the Princess Mary of the crown. Lady Jane was still too obscure for anyone outside the Court circle to imagine her succeeding, and in any case her mother had the prior claim. Meanwhile, de Scheyve was not taken in by Northumberland's attentions to the Princess, which were paid, he reported, in order to prove that he had no ambitions.[3] Nor was Mary deceived; she did not expect to obtain her inheritance without a struggle which might end in her own destruction.

That inheritance had sadly dwindled in value, if not in extent (Calais, Guines and Boulogne were still, at huge expense, in English hands), since the death of Henry VIII. In six years Somerset's wars, Northumberland's crooked policy and their satellites' frenzied lust for wealth and land had decimated the kingdom. The so-called Reformation had produced national bankruptcy and open corruption in all departments of State. The licentiousness and ignorance of the Protestant clergy surpassed the inefficacy and laziness of the Catholic priests and monks. (In one diocese, 171 out of 311 parsons could not repeat the Ten Commandments, ten could not say the Lord's Prayer and seven did not know who was its author, while sixty-two were pluralists and absentees.[4]) With few exceptions, the lawyers were frankly venal; the nobles were absorbed in their common feuds and rivalries for the accumulation of more property and vaster riches; the Army and the Navy were mutinous, inadequately provided for and irregularly paid. Finally, what were to prove the inestimable gifts of the English Prayer Book and Bible had, so far, merely created a speculative, irreverent, muddled and vaguely cynical attitude towards spiritual matters, vainly combated by such soldiers of Christ as Latimer, Ridley, Cranmer and Gilpin. For many, and those the most in need, God was now neither on the altar (had not the baker made Him?) nor in the next world. He had disappeared from everyday life in a cloud of argument, self-contradictions and senseless pillage. The whitewashed walls, once richly, if naively, painted with sacred stories, now bearing three lions rampant and a foolish motto in the language of the traditional enemy; the cracked single bell summoning the country folk to a service without magic, no better, some said, than a Christmas game: [5] the bare, secular tables in the middle of aisles where the children had sprawled and played during Mass: the smashed windows: the defaced screens: the empty niches – for kings and queens, bishops, martyrs and saints had perished together in the general holocaust – all these depredations had only helped to enrich the nobles, who were still enclosing the common land. Now they drank their French and Italian wines from gold and silver chalices; their antechambers were hung with embroidered copes and their furniture with jewelled altar-cloths; and their wives' and daughters' bared bosoms glittered with gems snatched from the Rood or from Our Lady's heavenly diadem.

The people from whom these treasures had been taken did not know, and if they had, would not have cared or understood that the wicked Duke, while unwittingly laying up death and degredation for himself, had also set in hand a movement which was to become one of England's glories and make her the wonder and envy of the world – and that within less than thirty years. In his efforts to rehabilitate the national finances and reduce unemployment Northumberland had organized trade expeditions to unexplored territories – Morocco, the Gold Coast, the Far East. From whatever motives (and they may well have been suspect) he started these schemes, he did carry them out, and with success. He formed a joint-stock company, to which the King gave letters patent. John Dee left his tutorship of Guilford Dudley to supervise the scientific side of the various ventures; Sebastian Cabot was employed as navigator; and the hazardous grandeurs of the British Empire were founded in the days of England's greatest poverty and weakness. [6]

Yet no one relying on the accounts of continental visitors could have guessed how miserably the people fared. Foreign residents were amazed, and indeed disgusted, by the luxurious habits and reckless expenditure of all classes. The reports of Etienne Perlin, a French priest, and of Battista Spinola, a Genoese merchant, combine in providing a unique and intimate view, not only of the English people but of Northumberland's plots and of Lady Jane's appearance in them. They coincide

with those of de Noailles, the French envoy, and Bishop
Godwin.

'This country', says Perlin, 'is very rich ... The people in
trade gain more in one week than people in Germany or Spain
gain in a month ... Even the artisans play tennis for crowns.'
He then comments on the price of food and the looks of the
natives (the men were 'handsome and ruddy', the women 'fair
as alabaster') and, while approving their generosity, love of
music and comfortable inns, deprecates their cruel punishments – why did they not break criminals on the wheel, as in
France? – their violence, rebelliousness and pride. The English
were as unreliable and dangerous as mad dogs. 'You will find
scarcely any noblemen,' he goes on, 'some of whose relations have not been beheaded ... While you see these great
lords in vast pomp and magnificence, the next instant you
behold them under the hands of the executioner.' Two typical
specimens of this class were '*le duc de Notembellant*' and
'*milor Suphor*', his principal ally. One of these *milors*, he was
not sure which, had a daughter, Madame Jeanne, in whom
Perlin did not take much interest.[7]

Spinola, who saw her only once, did. 'This Jana Groia,' he
reported, '. . . is very short and thin, but prettily shaped and
graceful. She has small features and a well-made nose, the
mouth flexible and the lips red. The eyebrows are arched and
darker than her hair, which is nearly red. Her eyes are spark-
ling . . . her colour good but freckled . . . In all, a charming
person ... very small and short.'[8]

De Noailles, who conversed with Jane, found her 'well
made', and was impressed by her '*esprit cultivé, dont la
modestie rehaussait extrêmement le mérite*'.[9] Bishop Godwin
was not at first much taken with her appearance. He thought
her features 'not admirable', ie, not striking, but considered
her 'handsome, incredibly learned, very quick-witted and wise
both beyond her sex and above her age'.[10]

In the years succeeding Jane's death the legend of her
beauty grew up and so held the public imagination that it was
accepted as true. An Italian, writing of her in Queen Elizabeth's reign, describes her as pretty, polite and attractive.[11] 'All

the graces in nature', says an eighteenth-century historian, 'conspired to improve the exquisite beauty of her face ... [She was] generally called the Queen of Hearts.'[12] This picture eventually developed into the vision popularized by Harrison Ainsworth in his novel *The Tower of London*, where he describes Lady Jane as tall, slender and 'gracefully bending' when in talk with an inferior.

Thus the real likeness was gradually obliterated from the public mind. The only English sixteenth-century picture of Lady Jane which exists (and even that is not absolutely authenticated), shows her as full-faced and sandy-haired – is this what Spinola meant by 'nearly red'? – with large, rather prominent brown eyes. The contemporary reports of her appearance and conversation give the impression that a lively, natural manner combined with youthful freshness to make her appear better-looking than she really was. She probably became thin, as Spinola saw her, soon after her marriage, when she fell ill and begged to stay on with her mother instead of joining Guilford and the Duchess of Northumberland at Durham House. This sickness, which Jane afterwards attributed to poison, so sure was she that the Dudleys had evil intentions, was perhaps a nervous disease. She seems to have thrown it off in June and to have succumbed to it again a few weeks later.[13]

During the six weeks that elapsed between her wedding and the King's death, Lady Jane remained in total obscurity, apparently unaware either that Edward might die at any moment or to what extent his demise must affect her. In view of the talk going on all round her, this seems hard to believe; and yet her own account of her state of mind, written during the third week in July, makes her non-acceptance of her situation perfectly clear.[14] She had been married to Guilford against her will: soon she would be his wife in fact as well as in name: she was sometimes ill: she was working at her languages and corresponding with Bullinger. This concatenation of circumstances may have resulted in an instinctive refusal to take in how important she had become, or in fact why she had been married to a Dudley. Certainly she had enough force of character to withdraw – as she had from the hunting parties at Bradgate – into her own world, and to stay there, until she was thrust out of it into that of her father-in-law and his fellow-conspirators.

Soon after the wedding Lady Jane and the Suffolks moved to Sheen, a palace on the river once belonging to Somerset, which before that had been a monastery. Some of the original occupants, no doubt incensed by the treatment they had received, were still hanging about the grounds; and eventually, hoping to drive out the Suffolks, they staged a threatening and bodeful apparition in one of the galleries. They waited till the Duke and Duchess were walking there; then, from an opening in the wall, a red hand appeared, brandishing a bloodstained axe.[15]

It is unlikely that the Suffolks accepted this crude demonstration as it was meant. In their world, a bloody axe was too familiar an object to be regarded as either a symbol or a warning.

ii

During the last days of May the King grew much worse, and it was thought that he must die within a fortnight, or less; no one believed that he would survive for another five weeks.[16] Northumberland had therefore to bring his plans to a head. He began by making Frances Suffolk promise that she would relinquish her claim to the throne in favour of Lady Jane (he seems to have done this before persuading Edward to alter the succession) and then commanding the consummation of Jane's and Guilford's marriage. The young couple were not publicly bedded; a reference to their situation in Jane's statement to Queen Mary makes it clear that some time between the end of May and the beginning of July they became, in every sense, husband and wife.[17]

Jane, who was now living at Durham House with Guilford and his mother, fell ill again. As she did not get better, the Duchess of Northumberland allowed her to go to the palace of Chelsea for what Jane afterwards described as a 'recreation' or cure. There she remained with the Duchess of Suffolk until Northumberland recalled her to her husband's side. She does not record the dates of these comings and goings, or mention Guilford, except as living with his mother; so it may be assumed that he did not visit her while she was in Chelsea.[18]

Northumberland now inaugurated a series of talks with Edward about the succession. The notion of cancelling Henry VIII's will and cutting out Mary and Elizabeth was not immediately acceptable; for Edward had the greatest reverence for his father's decrees, and a strong sense of propriety and order. So the Duke began by pointing out that, as soon as the Lady Mary succeeded she would enforce Popery on the nation, and the cause for which Edward had worked all his short life would perish. As the boy hesitated, he went on, 'It is the part of a religious and good prince to set apart all respects of blood, where God's glory and the subjects' weal may be endangered. That Your Majesty should do otherwise were, after this life – which is short –' he added with marked significance – 'to expect revenge at God's dreadful tribunal.'[19]

Edward, who longed for release from what he now described as 'this miserable life', was not proof against the threat of eternal damnation. He gave way: the Lady Mary should not succeed. But then – what of the Lady Elizabeth? She was a devout member of the Reformed Church; and apart from the fact that she was younger, her claim was equal to her half-sister's.

Northumberland was ready for that question. The Lady Mary, he said, 'could not be put by unless the Lady Elizabeth were put by also'. Their rights depended upon one another.[20] He went on to explain that either Princess, if she married a foreigner (and no other marriage was considered) would, by degrees, 'abolish all the ancient rights and immunities, till [her husband] extinguished at last the very name of England'. Edward seems to have remained silent. 'Your Majesty,' Northumberland urged in his most forceful and persuasive style, 'should consider again – and again. Kings owe protection to their subjects to defend them from injury. If they did not, divine vengeance would, some time or other, overtake them when, after the conclusion of this short life, they should stand before the judgement seat of God in order to receive the reward of everlasting life.'[21]

Edward agreed to eliminate his half-sisters. His logical mind then turned to the Lady Frances, as he still called her. If he died leaving no issue (for he still believed that he could recover) she might become Governess Regent of the kingdom.[22] Northumberland then summoned the Duchess of Suffolk, who in Edward's presence formally relinquished her claim to the Lady Jane.[23]

Within the next few days Northumberland's talks with the King took a different turn. He did not at once suggest that Edward should make a will leaving Lady Jane the crown. He dwelt, at what seems to have been considerable length, on the 'matchless qualities' of his little daughter-in-law and the 'agreeableness of her conversations with His Majesty's own affections'.[24] 'She hath imbibed the reformed religion with her milk,' he declared, 'and is married in England, to a husband of wealth and probity. Your Grace,' he went on, 'had always an affectionate sympathy with that excellent lady. You are bound by your duty to God to lay aside all natural affections to your father's house.'[25]

Northumberland then expatiated on the invalidity of the late King's marriages to Katharine of Aragon and Anne Boleyn respectively, and pointed out that, just as Henry VII had succeeded while his mother, Margaret Beaufort, was still alive, so the Lady Jane could take precedence of hers. He also instructed Edward's favourite companion, Henry Sidney, to 'entertain' his master with 'continued discourses of Lady Jane, the high esteem in which she was for her zeal and piety'.[26]

These conversations took place between May 30th and June 10th. At last the moment came when Northumberland was empowered by Edward to concoct the draft of the will. This the King copied out, with a shaking hand, under the heading of 'my devise for the succession'.[27] Northumberland then hastily assumed the role of the disinterested patriot and statesman. 'Although,' he said, 'the eldest of the three is married to my son, I am content that [Jane and Guilford] should be bound by oath to perform whatever Your Majesty should decree – for I have not so much regard to my own, as to the general good.'[28] He added, 'I do not consider so much mine own interest in the business, as the benefit of the whole kingdom.'[29]

So the terms of the will were roughed out, ready to be drawn up by the legal authorities. Edward, who had rallied, began to sink rapidly. Before he lost the use of his hand Northumberland suggested another alteration which, on or about June 10th, was incorporated into the final draft.

In the first draft, which was made before Edward realized that he was dying, he had contravened his father's arrangements by eliminating all female successors. This created an impossible situation, for there were seven women in line for the throne – Mary, Elizabeth, Frances Suffolk, her three daughters and Lady Margaret Clifford – and no males. His second draft eliminated Mary, Elizabeth and Frances and left the crown to 'the Lady Jane's heirs males'. In the third draft this sentence was altered to 'the Lady Jane *and* her heirs males'. (In his 'devise' the 's' is scratched out and the 'and' inserted above the line, the whole in the King's own hand.) In the event of Jane having no male issue, the succession came to Katherine Grey: if she had none, to Mary Grey, and if Mary Grey had none, to Margaret Clifford.[30]

This draft described the Princesses not only as illegitimate but as 'disabled ... to claim the said imperial crown', because they were 'but of the half-blood', adding that if either married a foreigner, his presence 'would tend to the utter subversion of the commonwealth of this our realm'.[31] Thus, by a plethora of objections, Edward, or rather Northumberland, destroyed the case against Mary and Elizabeth Tudor – for if they were illegitimate, then their marrying foreigners was of no importance.

In fact, at this point, Northumberland was beginning to lose his self-confidence and with it his ingenuity. So far, he had carried everything before him; now, both his actions and his speeches revealed a clumsiness and crudity which made the Council unwilling to proceed along the lines he had chosen. How many of them had seen the various drafts of the will before the final version was engrossed is not clear. Pembroke, Huntingdon, Winchester, Northampton, Arundel and Cranmer did; Winchester, Cranmer and Arundel objected to it on the grounds that although the power of bequeathing the crown had been granted to Henry VIII, a similar power could not be given to Edward VI without an Act of Parliament; therefore to subscribe to it amounted to high treason.[32] Northumberland overruled them, and proceeded with his plans.

Meanwhile, no one except the Council, and not all of them, knew what he was going to do. The French and Spanish Ambassadors were told nothing. Northumberland now paid the Princess Mary the attentions due to an heiress apparent; and the rumour went round that he was going to divorce his Duchess and marry the Lady Elizabeth himself. 'On every side,' de Scheyve reported, 'there are plans and preparations' – but for what? Such church furniture as remained was seized and sold. Suffolk and Northampton, accompanied by a party of gentlemen, visited Mary at Hunsdon in Hertfordshire in order to find out what supporters she had. Then de Scheyve was told that Northumberland's heir, the Earl of Warwick, was to be divorced in order to marry the Princess Elizabeth. On June 11th he wrote that a new Parliament had been called.[33] Still he could not arrive at a conclusion; still Northumberland reiterated his loyalty to Spain and his intention of abandoning France, and borrowed a large sum of money from the Emperor on the strength of this asseveration,[34] in order, de Scheyve believed, to bribe some lesser but important satellites; one was Sir John Gates, now Vice-Chamberlain and Captain of the King's Guard, another Sir Thomas Palmer, an experienced officer who had been one of the witnesses suborned to give evidence against Somerset.

Then, at last, de Scheyve began to guess at the truth. 'The Duke's and his party's designs to deprive the Lady Mary of the crown are only too plain', he reported. '... He will dissemble with the Princess till the King dies, and then make a *coup d'état* and kidnap her. He will say that her accession may bring ruin and establish Popery.' But: 'When it comes to the touch, Northumberland's party may desert him. He is hated and loathed for a tyrant, while the Princess is loved throughout the land. With her help, Northumberland may be worsted.'[35]

The Duke, aware of and indifferent to the people's hatred, sustained the part of the modest, hard-working minister in his speeches and letters, while using his rages to subdue those who withstood him. His instructions to Cecil abound with such phrases as 'I have scribbled my simple mind' and 'in my poor opinion'[36] and his appeals to the Lords were nobly inspiring. 'For the love of God,' he begged them, 'and the love which we ought to have to our master and country, let us be careful as becometh men of honour, truth and honesty ... that is, to be ready, not only to spend our goods, but our lands and lives ... and to despise the flattering of ourselves with heaping of riches upon riches, house upon house, building upon building ...'[37]

As the King grew daily weaker Northumberland may have felt that some of his own building was upon sand. He continued to issue announcements of Edward's improved health and gave a musical party for the Council.[38] When the French Ambassador, M du Boisdaulphin, made it clear that he was not prepared to put up with any more deception, Northumberland asked him and his suite to dine at Greenwich and visit His Majesty. After a great feast the envoys were ushered into an antechamber, where the Duke and some of the Councillors received them. Before M du Boisdaulphin could ask for an audience, Northumberland announced that his policy was, as ever, entirely French. Then, suddenly, his façade broke and, turning to the Ambassador, he said, 'What would your Lordship do in my case?' Du Boisdaulphin replied with a formal statement about his master's interests, adding that if the Lady Mary did not succeed, Henri II would advance the claims of his future daughter-in-law, Mary Stuart, thus indicating that Northumberland could count on his not coming to the Princess' help. Lady Jane and Guilford were not mentioned, and the envoys left without seeing Edward.[39]

Three and a half weeks before the King's death, his doctors told de Scheyve that he would be dead within three days.[40] This miscalculation caused Northumberland to hurry on the first stage of his *coup d'état*, and eventually helped to strengthen

Mary's position, which then seemed desperate: for she was isolated, apparently friendless and denied all access to her brother, whom she had visited for the last time four months ago.

On June 11th Sir Edward Montague the Lord Chief Justice, the Solicitor-General and the Attorney-General were summoned to Greenwich and ushered into Edward's bedchamber. Northumberland gave them the draft of his devise, and the King told them to make a deed of settlement on its terms. When they had read the scrawled pages, Montague, greatly troubled, said that without an Act of Parliament such a deed could have no validity. Edward, held up by his attendants, gasped out, 'I will hear of no objections', and desired them to proceed.[41]

Montague asked His Majesty's leave to withdraw in order to study the book, as it was called, at greater leisure, and he and the other judges returned to London. There, after some debate, they agreed that the devise was illegal and that to sign it would be treasonous. They were then summoned to Ely Place. As they waited in an antechamber an employee of Northumberland's entered and asked whether they had drawn up and signed the deed. Montague replied, 'I cannot. Such an act would be high treason.'

The door was flung open and Northumberland, white and shaking, burst in upon them. 'You are a traitor!' he shouted. 'I will fight with any man living in my shirt in this quarrel!' Montague, in his account of the scene, makes no secret of his terror; he and the others believed that their last hour had come.[42]

Next day they returned to Greenwich. As soon as they approached the bedside, now surrounded by Privy Councillors, Edward asked, 'Where are the letters patent? Why have they not been drawn?' He then fiercely ordered Montague, on his allegiance, to 'make quick dispatch', adding that he intended to call a Parliament immediately. Montague, in tears, fell on his knees. 'I have served Your Majesty and Your Majesty's most noble father these nineteen years,' he sobbed. 'I am a weak old man and without comfort,' adding that he had seventeen children.

The dying King ignored this plea and reiterated his commands. Eventually Montague and his fellows gave in, asking only for a grant of pardon under the Great Seal. 'I will not suffer that licence to be sealed,' Northumberland interrupted. 'I will have no man in better case than myself.'

It was then agreed that a pardon should be issued for all who signed, and the three lawyers retired, 'with weeping eyes', to draw up the settlement.[43]

On the 21st Edward, the judges and the Privy Council signed the will. Their signatures were followed by those of the eldest sons of peers, the Officers of the Household, the Secretaries of State, the Knights of the Privy Chamber and the sheriffs: more than a hundred names. Still Northumberland did not trust his unwilling and shifty crew. He drew up an 'engagement', in which the Councillors promised to support the Lady Jane as Queen, 'to the uttermost of their power, and never at any time to swerve from it'. All but Arundel signed this document.[44]

Two days later the prayers for the Lady Mary and the Lady Elizabeth were omitted in the London churches. On June 28th Northumberland entered into a secret arrangement with France (it was thought that he had agreed to sell Calais and Boulogne), raised a forced loan of £50,000 from the City, spaced his troops out over the country, and made his cousin, Sir Henry Dudley, second-in-command of the fleet under Sir Humphrey Clinton, another ally. Robert Dudley was sent with 300 horse to capture Mary; but she withdrew to Framlingham in Norfolk before he arrived. Elizabeth remained at Hatfield.[45]

Still no one, outside the Council and the Household, knew what conditions were contained in the will. De Scheyve thought that Jane might be proclaimed, and then rejected the idea. No woman, least of all a girl of fifteen, could succeed. Guilford Dudley was to be King, he told the Emperor, and did not even mention Jane in his report of the 27th. 'Northumberland's designs are obvious,' he concluded, 'God wishes to punish the kingdom.'[46]

Northumberland saw that there was only one thing to be done. He must keep the King alive while he seized the Princesses. He therefore dismissed the physicians who had looked after Edward since his infancy and installed his own doctor and a female quack, who declared herself perfectly able to cure His Majesty. She administered arsenic, which temporarily stopped the haemorrhages. While Edward began to suffer the agonies of poisoning, Mary and Elizabeth were summoned to receive his last commands. Their reactions were characteristic. Mary set off at once, and was turned back within a few hours of her doom by Sir Nicholas Throckmorton, an old enemy of the Duke. Elizabeth gave out that she was ill, and sent bulletins of her progress through her doctor.[47]

On or about July 3rd, when Edward was still conscious and praying for death, the quack was dismissed – perhaps murdered, for she was never heard of again – and the Court physicians were reinstalled. Lady Jane, now at Chelsea with her mother, was visited by the Duchess of Northumberland, who announced, 'If God should call the King to His mercy; it will be needful for you to go immediately to the Tower. His Majesty hath made you heir to his realm.' She added that there was no hope of Edward's life.[48]

Jane wholly rejected these statements, almost, it would seem, as if they were part of the nightmare in which she was living. 'Which words,' she explained, 'being spoken to me thus unexpectedly, put me in great perturbation and greatly disturbed my mind – as yet soon after they oppressed me much more. But I, *making little account of these words*, delayed to go from my mother.'[49]

The Duchess of Northumberland then made a fearful scene with the Duchess of Suffolk. If she was going to keep her daughter, why did she not keep Guilford as well? Jane and Guilford should not be parted. Frances Suffolk, equally enraged, replied that she ought to be 'free from the charge' of both young people. Let Jane go to Durham House. She went there, but returned to Chelsea, presumably at her own request, for three nights, having once more fallen ill.[50]

By now Northumberland's dealings with the quack had leaked out, and it was concluded that he was poisoning the King deliberately. Edward's toes and fingers were gangrenous; still he lingered on. The Duke countered these rumours by hinting that the Lady Mary had 'overlooked' His Majesty during her last visit. His situation was desperate – for his victim had lived too long. Every day his hold on the Privy Council, the armed forces, even on the Suffolks, loosened and shifted.

Indeed it seemed as if the Tudors had troubled the Dudleys from the beginning. Henry VII, having raised the Duke's father high, had left him to the vengeance of Henry VIII. Mary and Elizabeth, recalcitrant, elusive and undesirably popular, were dangerous enemies. Frances Suffolk might yet prove a greater nuisance than her fool of a husband. And Edward VI, over-scrupulous, obstinate and difficult, now menaced Northumberland's last and greatest scheme by clinging to his miserable life.

Then deliverance came. In the late afternoon of July 6th, with a single prayer for mercy from his pitiless Protestant God, the last Tudor King rolled up his eyes, stretched out his poor maimed hands, and died. In the great storm that burst over London, Lady Jane became Queen of England.

If Northumberland had paused to consider her during those last terrible hours – which is unlikely – it would have been as a figurehead, a future breeder of Dudleys, a negligible quantity. Within three days he was to realize that she was none of these, and that he had to deal with yet another Tudor.

NOTES

1. *Acts of the Privy Council*, vol IV, p 266.
2. Carte, *History of England*, vol III, pp 274–5.
3. *Cal SP Spanish*, vol XI, p 53.
4. Pollard, *Political History of England*, p 73.
5. Strype, *Life of Cranmer*, App xl.
6. Williamson, *The Tudor Age*, pp 216–17.
7. *Antiquarian Repertory*, vol IV, pp 508–12.
8. Davey, *Lady Jane Grey and Her Times*, p 253.
9. Vertot, *Ambassades de MM de Noailles*, vol II, p 194.
10. Godwin, *Annals of England*, p 264.
11. Pollini, *Historia Ecclesiastica*, p 351.
12. Carte, vol III, p 276.
13. Pollini, pp 260–97.
14. Ibid.

15. Strickland, *Lives of the Tudor and Stuart Princesses*, p 88.
16. *Cal SP Spanish*, vol XI, p 40.
17. Pollini, pp 260–97.
18. Ibid.
19. Godwin, p 255.
20. Baker, *Chronicle*, p 84.
21. De Thou, *History of His Own Time*, vol I, pp 602–3.
22. Turner, *History of England*, vol II, p 205.
23. Vertot, vol. II, p 205.
24. Heylyn, *History of the Reformation*, p 150; de Thou, vol I, pp 602–3.
25. Ibid, p 150.
26. Ibid.
27. Chapman, *The Last Tudor King*, p 272.
28. Godwin, p 256.
29. De Thou, vol I, p 603.
30. *Queen Jane and Queen Mary*, ed Nichols, pp 92–3.
31. Ibid.
32. Froude, *History of England*, vol V, p 162.
33. *Cal SP Spanish*, vol XI, pp 38, 40, 49.
34. Commendone, *Life of Graziani*, p 40.
35. *Cal SP Spanish*, vol XI, p 49.
36. Tytler, *England under the Reigns of Edward VI and Mary*, vol II, pp 154–6.
37. Froude, vol V, p 109.
38. Griffet, *Nouveaux Eclaircissements sur l'Histoire de Marie Reine d'Angleterre*, p 11.
39. Ibid; *Cal SP Spanish*, vol XI, p 53.
40. Ibid, p 32.
41. Chapman, *The Last Tudor King*, pp 280–2.
42. Ibid.
43. Ibid.
44. Froude, vol V, p 171.
45. *Cal SP Spanish*, vol XI, p 65.
46. Ibid, p 67.
47. Vertot, vol II, p 208.
48. Pollini, pp 260–97.
49. Ibid.
50. Ibid.

Chapter 4

The Accession of Lady Jane

A FEW days after the death of Edward VI, John Dove, constable of West Witham, was talking to Troughton, the town bailiff, at the common watering-place. A neighbour, James Pratt, who had been away, passed by, and Troughton called out to him, 'How like you the new scoured watering-place?' 'I like it well,' Pratt replied, 'and desire God to thank the doers thereof.' After some further conversation on what concerned them most, Pratt said, 'What news have you of King Edward?' Troughton, as became his official status, decided on discretion. 'None at all,' he said. 'The King is dead,' said Pratt, 'and you know it well enough.' 'I knew it not,' Troughton declared. 'How knew you His Grace to be departed?' 'It is true,' Pratt persisted, 'for the Queen's Highness is fled into Norfolk.'

As the three men stared at one another, Troughton burst out, 'O woe worth that villain that ever he was born, for his father was a traitor, and he is a very villain! His father would have killed the King's father.' Drawing his dagger, he went on, 'I wish this at the villain's heart – face to face, and body to body! God's plague light on him, that he may have a short life! I pray God to deliver the Queen's Majesty, and deliver Her Grace from him!'

Dove interrupted this discourse by pulling Troughton's coat-sleeve and drawing him aside. 'I would speak with you,' he whispered, and as they left Pratt by the watering-place Troughton put away his dagger. 'Beware what you say against the Duke,' urged the constable, 'for you know Pratt is not your friend, and he will make the worst of it.'

Troughton refused to be intimidated, and again drew out

his weapon. 'I have said, and I will say it whilst I live,' he shouted, 'you will shortly see him come to his father's death, and so I trust he shall—' and bidding them farewell, strode away across the common.[1]

Such talk was indeed extremely dangerous; but in the days immediately following Edward's death the Duke had no time to deal with informers. First, what was to be done with the King's body? The autopsy that must precede the embalming might reveal symptoms which would confirm suspicion of poison. Either the embalmers must be bribed – a risky business – or another body substituted for the rotting corpse of the boy who had been known as England's Treasure and Henry VIII's 'most precious jewel'.

No one knew exactly what Northumberland arranged. A few weeks later one of his sons said that the Duke, not daring to let Edward lie in state, had 'buried him privately in a paddock adjoining the Palace, and substituted in his place, to be seen by the people, a young man not very unlike him, whom they had murdered'.[2]

It is improbable that at this point and in these circumstances Northumberland could either have ordered or concealed the murder. Yet it may be that the bones now lying beneath the altar of the Chapel of Henry VII in Westminster Abbey are not Edward VI's, and that his dust has been disseminated in the suburbs of Greenwich. Northumberland's first plan was to conceal his death for a fortnight, leaving him where he was. The weather and the state of the corpse made this impossible, and Edward, or another, was disembowelled and coffined immediately. No one saw the body or reported on it. Henry Sidney, in whose arms Edward died, Christopher Salmon his valet and Dr Wroth, who were at his bedside on the afternoon of July 6th, made no statements, then or later. Sidney's comments on his master's death contain no indication of anything untoward having taken place; but he was a servant of the State and an ambitious courtier, whose marriage to Mary Dudley placed him under a cloud after Queen Mary's accession. Nothing was said, and the fate of the King's corpse remains uncertain. In due course – exactly when, is not clear – the coffin was conveyed to Westminster Abbey in the custody of twelve nobles, who kept watch over it in shifts, 'without torches or tapers', to the horror of the foreign Ambassadors.[3]

Meanwhile Lady Jane remained ignorant of her cousin's death. De Scheyve's spies reported it to him on the 7th.[4] The first persons to be officially informed were the Lord Mayor and the sheriffs, who were summoned to Greenwich on that day. They did not see the body, and no public announcement was made. On the 8th the news was conveyed to the Princesses, and that morning was occupied by Northumberland in further strengthening the armaments and fortifications of the Tower. De Scheyve's report to the Emperor outlines the situation. All the forces of the country were in the Duke's hands. Mary, although in great danger, had decided to make her claim to the throne by appealing to the people. This would be a mistake, for her position was in fact hopeless. De Scheyve sent a message urging her to give in; he believed that Northumberland, whose rule had now been firmly established, was bound to triumph. She should therefore submit herself to him, while de Scheyve promised him Spanish support. 'Possession of power,' he concluded in his report to the Emperor, 'is a matter of great importance, especially among barbarians like the English.'[5] The French envoys shared this view; they decided to abandon the Princess and subscribe to Northumberland's jurisdiction and the acceptance of Guilford as king. It occurred to neither party that Jane might be proclaimed,[6] in spite of the fact that the Lord Mayor and the City fathers, although sworn to keep the King's death secret, had taken the oath to her as their new sovereign.

On the 7th Sir John Gates summoned the Palace Guard, told them of the King's death and his will, and desired them to swear allegiance to Queen Jane. He added that their oath was 'to the Crown of England'. (This, when he heard of it, confirmed de Scheyve's belief that Guilford was to be proclaimed.) Gates went on to explain that the Lady Mary was not fit to succeed for three reasons: her mother's divorce from Henry VIII, her Catholicism and her sex.[7]

On the 8th Mary wrote a tactful and dignified letter to the

Council which reached them on the 9th. She began by assuming that she had succeeded and that they recognized her as Queen – although she found it 'strange' that she had not been informed of her brother's death until two days after the event. 'We shall and may,' she went on, 'conceive great trust, with much assurance in your loyalty and service, and therefore for the time interpret and take things not to the worst, that ye will, like noblemen, work the best. Nevertheless, we are not ignorant of your consultations to undo the provisions made for our preferment ... by whom, and to what end, God and you know; and nature cannot but fear some evil.' She concluded by appealing to their allegiance.[8]

On Sunday the 9th the Council, now completely subjugated and indeed terrorized by Northumberland, decided to inform Lady Jane of her accession and to proclaim her before telling Mary that she had no right to the throne and must acknowledge Jane as Queen. In the afternoon of that day they sent Mary Sidney to her at Chelsea, 'giving me to understand,' she says, 'that I must go that same night to Sion, to receive that which had been ordered for me by the King.'[9]

Jane, who was still suffering from what she believed to be the effects of poison, demurred, pleading sickness. Mary Sidney, who had her full share of the Dudley force of character, 'with extraordinary seriousness' replied: 'It is necessary for you to go with me.' The two girls then took barge to Sion House. Here the Northumberlands, Guilford, the Suffolks and the principal members of the Privy Council awaited them.

When the barge reached the water-gate Jane and Lady Sidney were received by the officers of the household. They entered the great hall, hung with tapestries and decorated with the spoils of innumerable churches, to find it empty. There they waited in silence.[10]

ii

'The Council,' says a contemporary historian, 'were as afraid of Northumberland as mice of a cat',[11] and another adds that 'by terror and promises' he had bound them to Lady Jane.[12]

Yet although they were apparently united behind him, the Duke knew that his situation would continue to be one of great danger until his daughter-in-law was crowned and Mary captured, in spite of the fact that he had command of the armed forces and the promise, at least, of French and Spanish support. Lady Jane's account of the scene at Sion House gives the impression that he dared not let his fellow-conspirators out of his sight. He was fairly sure of Suffolk, as being too scatter-brained and too deeply committed to threaten his power; but Northampton, Arundel, Huntingdon and Pembroke were ready, he knew, to go over to Mary if she succeeded in rallying the kingdom.

On the afternoon of July 9th this seemed unlikely. Some half-dozen nobles were in attendance on the Princess, but they had not called out their tenants; and the foreign Ambassadors appeared to be waiting on events. When Northumberland preceded the Councillors into the room where Mary Sidney and Lady Jane were waiting, he was still, it seems, testing their loyalty; for instead of telling her at once of Edward's death and her accession, he stood apart with Northampton and Arundel (were these the men he most distrusted?) while Huntingdon and Pembroke engaged Jane in a long conversation. These two nobles may have been told to prepare her for the official announcement. 'With unwonted caresses [compliments],' she says, 'they did me such reverence as was not at all suitable to my state.'[13]

She remained utterly bewildered. She knew that the King could not live much longer, and assumed that either Mary or Elizabeth would succeed. So when Huntingdon and Pembroke knelt to kiss her hand, she suspected that 'they were making semblance of honouring me', was deeply embarrassed, and blushed scarlet when one of them said something about her being 'their sovereign lady'.[14] In fact, she still did not understand, or rather, refused to take in, what these gestures and phrases might mean. It did not occur to her that such a cataclysmic event as Edward's death could have been concealed from her, his cousin, and from the general public.

This preliminary seemed endless. Shrinking and confused,

Jane could only submit until the Duke indicated that she, attended by Lady Sidney, should proceed to the Chamber of State, escorted by himself and the Lords.

There she found drawn up in order of precedence her father and mother, her husband, her mother-in-law and Lady Northampton. All did her reverence. Then Northumberland seems to have led her to a dais under the canopy reserved for royal personages.[15]

By this time she was in terror of she knew not what. Her account of the next few minutes creates an unforgettable picture: the slight, childish figure standing alone, gazing down with large, frightened eyes from one hard face to another – the Duke's, Guilford's, her parents' – while they stared back at her, unyielding, triumphant, tense.

Northumberland stepped forward. 'As President of the Council,' he began, 'I do now declare the death of His most blessed and gracious Majesty King Edward VI.' He then spoke at length of his and the nation's grief. 'But,' he went on, 'we have cause to rejoice for the virtuous and praiseworthy life that His Majesty hath led – as also for his very good death. Let us take comfort by praising his prudence and goodness, and for the very great care he hath taken of his kingdom at the close of his life, having prayed God to defend it from the Popish faith, and to deliver it from the rule of his evil sisters.'[16]

Lady Jane says nothing of her feelings at this point. She was perhaps still trying to take in the disaster of Edward's death as Northumberland continued. 'His Majesty hath well weighed an Act of Parliament,' the harsh voice went on, 'wherein it was already resolved that whosoever should acknowledge the Lady Mary or the Lady Elizabeth and receive them as heirs of the crown should be had for traitors, one of them having formerly been disobedient to His Majesty's father King Henry VIII, and also to himself, concerning the true religion. Wherefore in no manner did His Grace wish that they should be his heirs – he being in every way able to disinherit them.'[17]

In the silence that followed Lady Jane began to tremble. Northumberland concluded with dramatic brevity, 'His Majesty hath named Your Grace as the heir to the crown of

England. Your sisters will succeed you in the case of your default of issue.'[18]

Lady Jane, who describes herself as 'stupefied and troubled', was unable to speak.[19] Northumberland proceeded with his monologue, taking her cooperation for granted. 'This declaration,' he continued, 'hath been approved by all the Lords of the Council, most of the peers and all the judges of the land, and all this confirmed and ratified by letters patent under the Great Seal of England. There is nothing wanting but Your Grace's grateful acceptance of the high estate which God Almighty, the sovereign and disposer of all crowns and sceptres – never sufficiently to be thanked by you for so great a mercy – hath advanced to you.' He may have paused here for some acknowledgement; receiving none, he went on in what seems to have been his intimidating manner, 'Therefore you should cheerfully take upon you the name, title and estates of Queen of England, France and Ireland, with all the royalties and pre-eminences to the same belonging; receiving at our hands the first-fruits of our humble duty – now tendered to you upon our knees – which shortly will be paid to you by the rest of the kingdom.'[20] As they all knelt, he wound up: 'So these Lords render to Your Grace the honour which is due to your person. It becomes them,' he added significantly, 'in the best manner, that which, with deliberate mind, they have promised to the King, even to shed their blood, exposing their own lives to death.'[21]

A deadly faintness and nausea had been creeping over Lady Jane as the shock of Edward's death was overborne by the more fearful news of the greatness thrust upon her. She swayed and fell. Her own account of the next few minutes is necessarily confused; she gives the impression that, although partially overcome, she yet grasped her situation. She had been suddenly involved in a wrong which might end in some hideous disaster; and she was surrounded by a band of implacable intriguers. Then grief broke in upon fear. She burst into tears.[22]

Northumberland made no move to raise her, and nor did anyone else. Between her sobs she said something about 'so noble a prince',[23] while they waited for her to calm down – for these expressions of sorrow were perfectly in order – and to play her part in the scene. At last she spoke; and it was for them to be appalled. 'The crown,' she said, 'is not my right, and pleaseth me not. The Lady Mary is the rightful heir.'[24]

There is some doubt as to the Lords' reception of this extraordinary reply, the very last they had expected. Northumberland seems to have been the first to pull himself together; he spoke in violent anger.[25] 'Your Grace doth wrong to yourself,' he exclaimed, 'and to your house!' He then recapitulated the conditions of Edward's will. When he finished, the Duke and Duchess of Suffolk went into the attack; they commanded Jane on her obedience to do what was required of her.[26]

Still she held out, and Guilford Dudley – it may be at a look from his mother – intervened. According to de Noailles, who received a report of his behaviour from one of the Councillors, he attempted cajolery, 'sparing her neither prayers nor caresses'.[27]

These had as little effect as Northumberland's rage; but Lady Jane, who knew herself bound to honour the parents she feared and detested, had been halted by their appeal. It could not be God's wish that she should disobey them; so she asked Him what she should do. A few moments passed. There was no answer.[28]

According to her own account, Jane took this silence for permission to accept the crown, and shortly afterwards realized that she had been wrong to do so. She knelt and asked for guidance, 'humbly praying and beseeching'. 'If what hath been given to me is lawfully mine,' she said, 'may Thy Divine Majesty grant me such spirit and grace that I may govern to Thy glory and service, to the advantage of this realm.'[29]

So it ended. They came forward, one by one, and kissing her hand, swore allegiance, 'even to the death'. Lady Jane made some further protest about her own 'insufficiency', and then submitted.[30] Her assessment of her share in what she later perceived to be 'the common disgrace and shame of all' is judicial and detached. 'It did not become me to accept [the crown],' she says, adding that to do so showed 'a want of prudence'.[31]

Lady Jane's peculiar temperament is perfectly illustrated by this restrained yet merciless description of an agonizing ordeal. Her behaviour during the first forty-eight hours of her reign shows an equally characteristic simplicity and directness. She had consented to become Queen of England. Although that consent had been given under pressure, it was nevertheless the act of an independent and responsible person. Therefore she must now, with God's help, behave as a queen should. On this point, as on all others, she knew exactly what she ought to do – and what she intended to do.

NOTES

1. Howard, *Life of Lady Jane Grey*, p 307.
2. Parker Society, *Original Letters*, vol I, p 454.
3. De Thou, *History of His Own Time*, p 605.
4. *Cal SP Spanish*, vol XI, p 73.
5. Ibid.
6. Vertot, *Ambassades de MM de Noailles*, vol II, p 55.
7. Tytler, *England under the Reigns of Edward VI and Mary*, vol II, p 187.
8. Heylyn, *History of the Reformation*, p 157.
9. Pollini, *Historia Ecclesiastica*, pp 260–97.
10. Ibid.
11. Florio, *Historia de la vita ... Giovanna Graia*, p 35.
12. Godwin, *Annals of England*, p 264.
13. Pollini, ibid.
14. Ibid.
15. Ibid.
16. Ibid.
17. Ibid.
18. Ibid.
19. Ibid.
20. Heylyn, p 162.
21. Pollini, ibid.
22. Ibid.
23. Ibid.
24. Vertot, vol II, p 211.
25. Ibid.
26. Ibid.
27. Ibid.

28. Raviglio Rosso, p 56.
29. Pollini, ibid.
30. Ibid.
31. Ibid.

Part III

The Months of Martyrdom

> Violence is risen up into a rod of wickedness ... They
> have blown the trumpet, even to make all ready; but
> none goeth to the battle.
>
> *Ezekiel* vii. 11, 14

Frances Brandon, Duchess of Suffolk (1517-70) with her second
husband, Henry Grey (?-1554) – Lady Jane Grey's parents.
By Hans Eworth

Bradgate Manor, Leicestershire. The birthplace of Lady Jane Grey.
From an engraving by L. Knyff (1650-1721)

Queen Mary (1516–58). She became the fourth Tudor monarch and was the daughter of Henry VIII. *By Antonio Moro*

Henry Fitzalan, 12th Earl of Arundel (1511?–80). He warned Mary
of Northumberland's plot to exclude her from the succession.
From the studio of Steven van der Meulen

Sir Thomas Wyatt
(1521 ?–54), son of the
poet. He led an
insurrection against
Mary's marriage to
Philip of Spain and tried
unsuccessfully to restore
Lady Jane Grey to the
throne. *By an unknown
artist after a portrait of
about 1550*

John Dudley, Duke of
Northumberland (1502 ?–
1553). Lady Jane Grey was
married to Guilford
Dudley, his son, and he
tried to manoeuvre Lady
Jane Grey onto the
throne to gain power.
By an unknown artist

Chapter I

The Rival Queens

T H E scene which culminated in Lady Jane's acceptance of the crown lasted until the early evening of July 9th. Nothing more could be done before daybreak; but there were many arrangements to be made, the first of which was that the public announcement of the King's death should be immediately followed by the proclamation of the new Queen, while this coincided with her entry into the Tower as the reigning sovereign. All the details had been settled beforehand, even to the order of the barges conveying her, her family and the Council, down the river. The crown jewels had been set out and the state apartments prepared to receive her. Then an unexpected difficulty arose.

Struggling under his enormous burden of suspense, administration and intrigue, Northumberland had not considered Jane as an individual. Their intercourse remained formal and almost meaningless (to him, at least) until she refused the crown; but even that set-back, although it must have disturbed him, had been momentary and could now be disregarded. Any trouble in that quarter – and there was little or nothing to fear from a well-trained girl of fifteen – was the business of the Suffolks, the allies on whom he most relied.

Yet it seems as if Lady Jane's strange and inconvenient behaviour had suddenly illuminated not only her personality but her appearance – for at some point during the final preparations it became clear that when she stepped out of the barge her tiny figure would be almost invisible to the crowds gathered on the opposite bank. The people had hardly seen her, and knew nothing of her except that she was the daughter-in-law of the most hated man in England. She must be raised, literally, from this unsuitable obscurity – what was to be done?

At last someone suggested putting her into chopines – three-inch wooden clogs – and they were strapped under her shoes. Her brocaded kirtle and long-sleeved bodice were of the Tudor colours – white and green – embroidered with gold. Her white coif was set with emeralds, diamonds, rubies and pearls. Guilford also must be gorgeous; they dressed him in a doublet and hose of white and gold which set off his height and fairness. As Lady Jane stepped into the barge the chopines were revealed; but her dress would conceal them during the walk from the water-gate to the main entrance of the Tower.[1] These, the last touches to the outward show of the *coup d'état*, were completed by the early afternoon of the 10th. Between three and four o'clock the procession was on its way.

The storms following the King's death had changed to still, bright weather, so that the panorama of the Thames, gloriously revealed, might have been especially designed to display the gilded state barges, each with its complement of uniformed rowers and glittering personages. Jewelled caps, swords and billaments caught and threw back the sunlight; gold and silver tissues, multicoloured damasks, the smouldering richness of red and blue and lilac velvet became kaleidoscopic as the barges slid over the water and the clear drops flashed and fell from the oars in transient brilliance, constantly renewed and regularly demolished with each steady stroke of the blade. As they swept past the meadows of Isleworth and between the shining Hounslow marshes, beyond Chelsea Reach and below the Bridge of the Knights into the City of Westminster, there, along the left bank, majestically towering above the brown, red and cream-colour of the little houses, stood the silvery-grey palaces which were the background of their adventure – Arundel House, Baynard's Castle, Suffolk House, Holborn, Ely Place, Westminster Hall.

After they shot London Bridge and passed Billingsgate and the Custom-House the cannon thundered a salute. It was as well, perhaps, that the noise was deafening; for from the banks, thronged with staring people, there came no sound at all.[2] Those who, that morning, had heard that their adored King was dead and listened to the proclamation of his unknown,

unwanted cousin, gazed in angry resentment at what they
thought of as that villain's progress. They hated him now
more than ever; for he had dared to set this puppet girl above
the Lady Mary, and bribed a handful of archers to shout and
fling up their caps when the heralds declared her Jane by the
Grace of God Queen of England, Ireland and France, Defen-
der of the Faith and of the Church the Supreme Head on earth.
Their Queen was King Harry's daughter; no other should take
her place.[3]

So only one of those who watched Jane and her Court dis-
embark troubled to describe her appearance. The English
chroniclers and diarists recorded the fact and her reception
without comment and as if in cold disgust.[4] But Battista Spinola, who must have been standing very near, observed her
closely, and noted every detail of her dress and features. In
spite of her freckles, her small stature and her thinness, he
found her pleasing – 'graceful and well made.' Her colouring
was clear and healthy; 'and when she smiled, she showed her
teeth, which are white and sharp. In all,' he concluded, *'una
persona graziosa e animata.'* [5]

The Genoese merchant's meticulous account makes it clear
that Lady Jane had recovered from the shock and terror of the
day before. Indeed, no young and high-spirited girl, however
sensitive, scrupulous and modest, could have shrunk from or
rejected the splendours she was now enjoying. Long ago, as it
must have seemed to her, she had very nearly become Queen
Consort – and such a possibility is not easily forgotten or discounted. The vitality of youth, the animation and pleasure
caused by the knowledge that she was the central figure of an
historic event, made her as radiant as a queen ought to be. And
the fact that her mother was carrying her train – that six of the
greatest nobles in England supported the canopy under which
she walked – that the comely and graceful Guilford, cap in
hand and bowing low at every other step, paid her, as Spinola
observed, 'much attention' – all these tributes called for and
obtained an agreeable and lively response. So she entered the
palace of the Angevin, Plantagenet and Tudor kings as if it
were her own – dignified, confident and serene.

On the threshold stood the Marquess of Winchester and Sir John Bridges, the Lieutenant of the Tower, surrounded by civilian and military officials and backed by the Yeomen of the Guard, each with his gilded axe over his shoulder. As Winchester knelt to present the keys of the fortress, Northumberland stepped forward, took them from him and himself gave them to his daughter-in-law, thus making it clear from whom her power derived.[6] The ravens croaked and fluttered. The guns crackled and roared; smoke enveloped the turrets, veiling their gilded cupolas and silken flags. Bowing courtiers and statesmen, kneeling pages, curtsying ladies, lined the slope leading up to the White Tower and the royal apartments. So, passing the dark, squat chapel of St Peter-ad-Vincula and the empty, sunny square of Tower Green, Lady Jane entered into the stronghold which was all her kingdom – never to leave it again.

Today, William the Conqueror's White Tower looks much as it did when Lady Jane entered it four hundred years ago – gracefully soaring yet solidly compact, noble yet unpretentious, and so proportioned as to dominate the surrounding structures. After nine and a half centuries its dazzling whiteness has darkened to pearl grey; but from a distance the effect is still one of clear, unshadowed colour and subtly decorative strength. The architect, a monk from Bec, while designing an impregnable fortress, enriched what was then known as the Keep with luxurious amenities: large state rooms, wide doorways, high, narrow windows and an exquisite little chapel occupying the centre of the second and third floors. St John's is one of the oldest, best preserved and most beautiful buildings in England. Its plain round columns supporting a clerestory lighted by a second tier of windows are encircled by an ambulatory, the whole surmounting crypts which in Lady Jane's day were used as dungeons.

Then, as now, it must have produced a haunting melancholy. Here Henry VI said his last prayers before he was murdered: here the vanquished Duc d'Orléans heard Mass after being captured at Agincourt; in the room below, Richard II signed his abdication; and under a staircase on the south side were thrust the bodies of Edward V and his six-year-old brother of York, who 'disappeared' in the reign of Richard III.

When Lady Jane and her Court attended their first service they found the chapel as bare of ornament as it is now. The wall-paintings given by Henry III had been whitewashed, the medieval stained glass smashed or wrenched away; instead of the altar a table was placed in the aisle. Only the carved capitals, with their fluid, T-shaped figures remained as memorials of rejected faith and Norman elegance.

When they descended to the presence-chamber, Lady Jane took her place under the state canopy, presumably in order to receive the homage of the Tower dignitaries. But first, her claim must be assured in another way. Northumberland, having given Winchester his instructions, left him in charge of the proceedings. Lady Jane, with her husband and some few attendants – among whom were her old nurse Mrs Ellen, and Mrs Tilney, her gentlewoman – seem to have waited there while the Councillors composed a reply to the Princess Mary's letter in another room. Then Winchester also left, but not to join them. He returned carrying a quantity of jewels and the Crown Imperial of the realm.

ii

More than a hundred years before Lady Jane was proclaimed, the slender circlet of the early Plantagenet kings had been replaced by the 'closed' Crown Imperial. (This pattern of crown was worn by Queen Elizabeth II in 1953.) After 1649 it was broken up and remodelled for three monarchs – Charles II, George IV and Queen Victoria; but the design – an arched diadem surrounded by fleur-de-lys, culminating in an orb and cross and encircling a velvet cap – has not greatly varied between Lady Jane's day and the present time. According to a contemporary, its shape symbolized the reformed faith. 'The Crown of England,' said Bishop Tunstall to Henry VIII, 'is an Empire of itself, much better than now [is] the Empire of Rome; for which cause Your Grace weareth a close crown.'[7] Its two historic jewels – the Black Prince's ruby and the sapphire of Edward the Confessor – displayed, and nearly lost, by Henry V at Agincourt and by Richard III on Bosworth Field, were rather more prominent in Lady Jane's time than now, because the crown is larger and richer than when Lord Derby rescued it from a thorn-bush and set it on her great-grandfather's head. Yet as she saw it, in the presence-chamber of the White Tower, so it can be seen today – an extraordinary emblem of hierarchic and sanctified power.

And so indeed she regarded it. For her, it symbolized, not merely rank and dominion, but a whole system of political and religious belief. The Crown stood for the State and the con-stitution – and all three were sacred. That it should be handled, much less worn, by an unauthorized person and without the accompanying ceremonies, struck her as a kind of blasphemy, for she had been brought up on the Tudor theory of majesty. A crowned and anointed monarch stood for God on earth; such persons received their rights through God and from the people, as represented in Parliament. From the moment that this power was bestowed the monarch became absolute: but it must be bestowed in the proper manner.

Lady Jane's account of Winchester's attempt to establish her status shows that she returned to the mood of the day before – one of suspicion, anxiety and terror. She seems to have ac-cepted, although with misgiving, the gold chain with forty clusters of pearls set in gold, the bracelets and the emerald and diamond necklaces, for they were not part of the regalia.[8] But, 'the Crown,' she says, 'had never been demanded ... by me, or by anyone in my name,' and she refused it. Winchester 'further wished me to put it on my head, to try whether it became me or no. The which, although with many excuses, I refused to do.' 'Your Grace may take it without fear,' the Lord Treasurer as-sured her, and at last she consented to let him put it on, 'to see how it fitted.' He said, 'Another shall be made to crown your husband withal.'[9]

Then the inner range and meaning of the plot of which she was the central figure revealed itself to Lady Jane. 'Which thing,' she goes on, 'I for my part heard truly with a troubled mind and with ill will, even with infinite grief and displeasure of heart.'[10] There she stood, crowned, Northumberland's daughter-in-law, Guilford's wife, the tool of the one, the benefactress of the other – and nothing more.

Winchester went away, followed by everyone else except Guilford. To him, the issue was simple. His all-powerful father had married him to Jane so that she should make him King of England, and now the moment had come for her to do so. She refused. Only Parliament, she said, could give him that position. 'I will be made King by you and by Act of Parliament,' he persisted childishly. Again she denied him, and a furious argument ensued. Lady Jane was unshakeable. Guilford, bursting into tears, rushed from the room to find his mother. Lady Jane was left alone.[11]

A few minutes later she roused herself to send for Pembroke and Arundel. To them she spoke with calm authority and characteristic caution. 'If the crown belongs to me,' she said, 'I would be content to make my husband a duke. But I will never consent to make him King.' Before the lords could reply Guilford and the Duchess of Northumberland returned. To the spoilt boy's reproaches and his mother's enraged abuse the fifteen-year-old Queen of an hour made the same answer. She would do nothing unconstitutional: she would not act without the consent of Parliament. As the Duchess continued to storm and rave and Guilford to lament, she repeated her promise to make him a duke – of Clarence, if he so desired. 'I will not be a duke, I will be King,' he petulantly replied, and again his mother intervened. 'You shall no longer sleep with her,' she exclaimed, and adding that they would instantly return to Sion House, she swept him from the room.[12]

Jane turned to Arundel and Pembroke and commanded them to fetch Guilford back. He must not leave. His place was by her side, whether he shared her bed, 'as formerly,' or not. They obeyed her – and so did Guilford and his mother. Lady Jane sums up the situation with her usual detachment and restraint. 'And thus,' she concludes, 'was I deceived by the Duke and the Council, and ill treated by my husband and his mother.'[13]

She now knew herself trapped, perhaps doomed. Thenceforward, according to a seventeenth-century historian, 'she always feared that there stood a scaffold secretly behind the throne.'[14] Common sense and realism, rather than modesty or maidenly shyness, had made her hesitate to accept the crown. Having accepted it, however wrongly, she would not go back from her decision. She continued to exercise her prerogative. And her personality, suddenly breaking out of the chrysalis of a harsh and repressive upbringing, was such that she did so with complete success. No one questioned her right to give certain orders. Meanwhile, she confined herself to giving those she knew could be carried out. She did not attempt to interfere with arrangements and plans of which she had neither knowledge nor control. This attitude, typical of the Tudor genius, seems to have been adopted from the moment that the crown was placed on her head. So, between the hours of four and seven on the afternoon of July 10th, the first of her reign, Lady Jane's metamorphosis was achieved. She ceased to protest; she either remained silent or issued her commands.

iii

The Lords' reply to the Princess Mary's assumption that she had succeeded, composed by Northumberland, was designed to commit them irrevocably to his cause. If that cause was defeated – on the evening of the 10th this seemed virtually impossible – and she became Queen, they would be self-condemned of high treason. They not only denounced her as a bastard by referring to her 'supposed title', but threatened to punish her if she did not at once submit herself to them and their 'sovereign lady Queen Jane ... If you will for respect show yourself quiet and obedient (as you ought), you shall find us ... ready to do any service that we with our duty may, and to be glad of your quietness, to preserve the common state of this realm.'[15]

One subordinate but far-sighted member of the Council managed to avoid signing this document. Sir William Cecil used his position as Northumberland's secretary to keep in touch with Mary through Sir Nicholas Throckmorton and his own secretary, Alford. When it was suggested that Cecil should draw up the proclamation of Lady Jane, he replied, 'They shall

draw it who list,' in Alford's presence, afterwards citing him as
a witness. Northumberland seems not to have noticed Cecil's
attitude. Arundel did, and began to consider adopting the same
tactics; he was still determined to revenge his imprisonment
after Somerset's trial. He attached himself to Cecil, and they
became allies.[16]

Meanwhile, it was obvious that the Council's first proclamation had not sufficed. The people's response was such that it
was decided to approach them again, in a more placatory manner. Heralds were sent out once more, in London and the provinces, to repeat the news of Edward's death, his will and Lady
Jane's entry into the Tower 'as rightful Queen of this realm . . .'
The proclamation continued: 'We therefore will you to understand . . . that you will endeavour yourself in all things to the
uttermost of your power, not only to defend our just title, but
also to assist us in our rightful possession of this kingdom, and
to disturb, repel and resist the feigned and untrue claim of the
Lady Mary, bastard daughter of our great-uncle King Henry
VIII of famous memory.'[17]

This second announcement was received by the Londoners
in cold silence, in spite of the fact that Queen Jane promised to
be 'most benign and gracious to all her people, and to maintain
God's holy word and the laws of the land'.[18] There were no
rejoicings. 'The people showed nothing but grief,' said a German eyewitness.[19] Another foreign resident, Etienne Perlin,
went out to note what was going on, and saw no demonstrations
and not a single bonfire.[20]

At Ludgate the heralds took up their station outside the St
John's Head tavern. The drawer, Gilbert Potter, was standing
there among a group of people. As the heralds concluded Potter
shouted, 'The Lady Mary hath the better title!', was denounced by his master and put in the pillory. He stood there all
day, pinned by the ears, which were cut off when he was released. It was later remarked, as a good omen for the Princess'
cause, that his employer was drowned shooting London Bridge
that same evening.[21]

A more discreet and much more powerful antagonist
watched and waited from within the Spanish Embassy. Simon

Renard, who had reached London on June 27th, reported to the Emperor daily and at length. This shrewd and sceptical observer, while detesting Northumberland and all he stood for, held out no hope of his defeat.

Indeed the Duke now felt himself secure enough to ignore the Imperial envoys. He did not inform them of the King's death till four days after it took place, when de Scheyve and Renard received the news as ordinary members of the public – a marked discourtesy, indicating that they had no influence. Although they were asked for assurances of their master's friendship, and something polite was said about good relations continuing between England and Spain, Northumberland did not see them himself, nor were they received by the new monarch.[22] On the morning of the 12th they still did not know that Lady Jane had been proclaimed. 'We have been told,' wrote Renard, 'that the new King and Queen are to be proclaimed this very day from the Tower of London and from Westminster.' All they could do was to beg the Council 'to be good to the Lady Mary', and wait for instructions from the Emperor. What ought they to do, for instance, if Guilford gave them audience? Mary's chances were so poor that they were prepared to accept him – but how? Spanish etiquette did not provide for an occasion of this kind. Then they heard – apparently in a roundabout manner – that Mary and Elizabeth had been declared illegitimate.[23]

They accepted the situation resignedly, as did de Noailles, who had been earlier informed. On the 10th he was writing of Guilford as 'the new King', and added that he was supporting Northumberland and confident of his success.[24]

Renard and de Scheyve waited in hopeless bewilderment as events rushed past them. When the Emperor's letter came it gave them little encouragement and must have increased their depression. They should pay court to Northumberland, he wrote, and discourage the Lady Mary from making any move. (They had in fact decided to leave unanswered the plea for help which she sent them from Framlingham on the 10th.) Meanwhile, relations must be established with the Dudley family. 'How many sons has this Duke, and are they well thought of?' the Emperor asked. 'Also, how many sisters has Suffolk's

daughter?' He added that it might be as well to consider the
Lady Elizabeth – what pretext had been used to debar her?[25]

The envoys replied to these questions with such information
as they had been able to collect, and tried to cheer up the Emperor by describing the gloom with which Lady Jane's proclamation was received. Then Northumberland announced
that Jane and Guilford would be crowned in Westminster
Abbey within a fortnight, and orders were given that they
should be served on the knee, while Guilford's pettishness was
assuaged by his being addressed as 'Your Grace'.[26] On the evening of the 10th, Jane, through Winchester, sent to the Master
of the Wardrobe at Westminster for twenty yards of velvet,
twenty-five ells of fine holland and three and three-quarter
ells of coarse holland cloth.[27] With these arrived a coffer which,
when opened, revealed a collection of oddments including
jewelled head-dresses, a gilt toothpick in the shape of a fish,
pearl buttons, a prayer book, some coins, a leather purse, eye-
brow tweezers, shaving-cloths, a broken ring – and a gold clock
which had belonged to the Duke of Somerset.[28]

On the 11th Ridley preached on Jane's behalf at St Paul's,
declaring Mary and Elizabeth bastards, to the grief and rage
of the congregation. The better-educated began to dispute Lady
Jane's rights. Some thought Mary Stuart should succeed.
Others said that the first Duke of Suffolk's grandchildren ought
to be excluded because he had not been legally divorced from
his third wife when he married Henry VIII's sister. 'But in
this ... the difference was great ... since [Mary and Elizabeth]
were declared bastards in law by Henry VIII ... whereas this
against Charles Brandon's issue was only a surmise.' It was
further (incorrectly) added that no mother had ever resigned
the crown to her daughter, as the Duchess of Suffolk had to
Lady Jane; but then, that was the result of Suffolk's feebleness
and Northumberland's ambition.[29] No one now dared speak
for the Lady Mary; to do so was to risk execution.[30]

So passed the first stage of the *coup d'état*. From the evening
of the 10th to that of the 11th there were no disturbances. The
Council, Lady Jane, Guilford and the Duchess of Suffolk and
Northumberland were at supper when a messenger arrived. He

brought a letter from Mary dated Sunday the 9th at Framlingham Castle. She wrote that she had proclaimed herself Queen, adjured the Councillors to avoid bloodshed, promised to respect the reformed faith and concluded, 'We require and charge you . . . on your allegiance, which you owe to God and us and none other, that for our honour and the surety of our realm, only you will employ yourselves; and forthwith, upon receipt hereof, cause our right and title to the crown and government of this realm to be proclaimed in our city of London, and such other places as to your wisdom shall seem good . . . not failing hereof, as our very trust is in you; and this our letter, signed with our own hand, shall be your sufficient warrant.'[31]

The letter was read aloud. A dead silence followed, broken by the sobs and lamentations of the two Duchesses. Lady Jane said nothing. After some discussion it was decided that the Earl of Warwick and Lord Robert Dudley should at once advance on Framlingham with a party of horse.[32]

The two brothers arrived on the 12th, and were completely routed, only just escaping with their lives. Mary, who had proclaimed her right when she had no more than fifteen gentlemen with her, was now at the head of an army. Her advance on London had begun.[33]

NOTES

1. Spinola's report, in Davey, p 252.
2. Godwin, *Annals of England*, p 264.
3. *Greyfriars Chronicle*, ed Nichols, pp 78–81; Strype, *Ecclesiastical Memorials*, vol III, pt 1, p 17; de Thou, *History of His Own Time*, p 605; *Cal SP Spanish*, vol XI, pp 77–89.
4. Ibid; Wriothesley's *Chronicle*, p 85.
5. Davey, p 252.
6. De Thou, p 606.
7. Jones, *Crowns and Coronations*, p 41.
8. Pollini, *Historia Ecclesiastica*, pp 260–97.
9. Ibid.
10. Ibid.
11. Ibid.
12. Ibid.

13. Ibid.

14. Heylyn, *History of the Reformation*, p 163.

15. Holinshed, *Chronicle*, vol III, p 1066.

16. Strype, *Annals*, vol I, pt 1, pp 485–7.

17. Losely MSS, pp 122–6.

18. Burnet, *History of the Reformation of the Church of England*, vol II, pt 1, p 368.

19. Parker Society, *Original Letters*, vol I, p 367.

20. *Antiquarian Repertory*, vol IV, p 503.

21. Holinshed, vol III, p 1065.

22. *Cal SP Spanish*, vol XI, pp 77–89.

23. Ibid.

24. Harbison, *Rival Ambassadors at the Court of Queen Mary*, p 47.

25. *Cal SP Spanish*, vol XI, pp 77–89.

26. Turner, *History of England*, vol II, p 217.

27. Nichols, *History of Leicestershire*, vol III, p 672.

28. Howard, *Life of Lady Jane Grey*, p 149.

29. Burnet, vol III, pt 1, p 283.

30. De Guaras, *The Accession of Queen Mary*, p 91.

31. Holinshed, vol III, pp 1066–71.

32. *Cal SP Spanish*, vol XI, pp 77–89.

33. Ibid.

Chapter 2

The Authority of Lady Jane

FROM the 10th to the 13th of July, life in the White Tower followed a set pattern. Mornings and afternoons were given up to Council meetings with a two-hour interval for dinner at midday. Lady Jane was not present at the conferences; Guilford was, sitting at the head of the table.[1] From Winchester or her father she then received the reports of Northumberland's decisions and signed such papers as were put before her. Secluded in the state apartments, she at first knew nothing of the Council's private intrigues and feuds. That Huntingdon was determined to outdo Suffolk, that Winchester had tried to withstand the alterations of Edward's will, that Pembroke had not yet allowed the marriage of her sister Katherine and his son to be consummated[2] and that Arundel would take the first opportunity to revenge himself on her father-in-law – all these aspects were revealed to her after her nine days' reign. With her gentlewomen and the two Duchesses she joined the Lords for meals, sitting under her canopy with Guilford and retiring immediately afterwards.[3] In that assembly this husband and wife must have looked startlingly, even pathetically, youthful. Theirs were the only unlined faces; now that Guilford had been pacified by the empty show of royalty, their opinions were not asked for, nor their wishes, if they expressed any, considered.

After four hundred years, the portraits of those surrounding Lady Jane and Guilford Dudley display, with one exception, a curious similarity, partly because mid-sixteenth-century fashions combine with stylized technique to disguise oddities and quirks of character. Thick, flowing beards and moustaches hide the mouths, the noses are long, the eyes narrow and deep-set, the colouring is neutral. The general effect is one of withdrawal, shiftiness and icy pride. Only Northumberland's picture shows him as he was – a cunning, witty, unabashed deceiver, who seems to know exactly what he wants, and who is as cynically indifferent to loathing as to flattery.

This terrifying study, the work of an anonymous artist, is still hanging in Sir Henry Sidney's manor-house of Penshurst, and is one of the least known and most vivid likenesses of the age. Although the painter was obviously not a great nor even a distinguished craftsman, the mingling of slyness, mockery and contempt with which the sitter eyed him gave his reproduction of these qualities an extraordinary power and conviction. Northumberland's colouring is coarsely healthy – and suspicion is thus aroused; did he rouge to disguise the pallor caused by overwork and nervous strain? The red, pouting, sensual mouth, the high, arched eyebrows, the neat, clipped beard which was not to become the mode till after his death – all these are in marked contrast to the drab, flattened aspect of his fellow-conspirators, as is the flamboyance of his dress. His black velvet surcoat is trimmed with sable, his scarlet doublet sets off the sapphire blue of his Garter ribbon; the white plume and the jewelled classical medallion in his cap draw attention to the cold merriment, the sharp jauntiness of his glance. The whole conveys a fearful certainty. So Northumberland must have appeared to those he bullied and subjugated, as also to the family who served him and defiantly reverenced his memory. 'My chiefest honour,' said his grandson Sir Philip Sidney, 'is to be a Dudley.'[4]

Of those he threatened and crushed, Lady Jane was the bravest and the most despairing. From the moment she realized that Northumberland had made her Queen so that Guilford should be King, she concluded that he was going to poison her in order to reign through his son. This was not the conviction of a distracted and hysterical girl, she attributed the falling out of her hair ('all my hair', she says, although there is no other record of her going bald[5]), her inflammation and the subsequent peeling of her skin, to the Northumberlands' machinations: and not unreasonably. They must have been exacerbated by her first refusing to marry Guilford and then making difficulties about the succession. That she had been overborne on both points did not detract from this maddening recalcitrance; and now she had added to the score against her by her refusal to crown their idolized boy and by the insulting offer of a dukedom. From Lady Jane's point of view – indeed, from the point of view of anyone in her circumstances and in that age – she had become an object of revenge. That her conclusions were mistaken does not make them foolish or far-fetched. Her situation was unspeakably horrible. If Northumberland's plot succeeded, she might be murdered; if it did not, she would be executed for high treason. In her terror, the fact that she and Guilford were intended to found a Dudley dynasty was forgotten. Meanwhile, Northumberland seems to have ignored her refusal to crown Guilford. No doubt he counted on being able to force her to do so when the time came; for there could be no coronation ceremony until Mary was defeated and captured.

The evening of the 11th and the morning and afternoon of the 12th were spent in organizing the Government forces and reissuing the proclamations in London and the provinces; in several districts the soldiers made the sheriffs proclaim Lady Jane two or three times in one day.[6] Northumberland then sent an envoy, Mr Shelley, to Charles V 'from our sovereign lady Queen Jane', announcing her accession. 'Ye shall understand,' the letter continued, 'that although the Lady Mary hath been written to from us to remain quiet, yet nevertheless we see her not so weigh the matter that if she might, she would disturb the state of this realm, having thereunto as yet no manner of help or comfort, but only the concurrence of a few lewd, base people; all the other nobility and gentlemen remaining in their duties to our sovereign lady ...'[7]

By the late afternoon of the 12th the preparations for an advance into East Anglia were complete, and a final conference was held. It was unanimously agreed that Suffolk should raise the country against the Princess, while Northumberland continued his administration from the capital. No one disputed this arrangement. Suffolk's popularity with the people and Northumberland's knowledge and skill made the division obvious and inevitable. The Lords then left Northumberland and waited on Lady Jane in order to tell her what had been decided and to obtain her signature for the various commissions. When she realized that Suffolk was leaving her in Northumberland's power she burst into tears. Then she declared herself. Northumberland must take the field. 'My father,' she said, 'must tarry at home in my company.'[8]

The Lords hesitated, considered – and submitted. Such ruthless potentates as these were utterly indifferent to the distress and terror of a fifteen-year-old girl. But they had made her their Queen and given her the powers of life and death; within forty-eight hours of her arrival at the Tower her letters had gone out to her 'good brothers' of France and Spain. Not only so: there was that in her personality which enforced obedience. The fact that she could have refused to sign the commissions unless they did as she told them, did not arise.

Faced with the task of breaking the news to Northumberland, the Lords returned to the Council Chamber and told him of the change of plan. Because he did not trust them out of his sight, his objections were numerous and prolonged. They resorted to flattery and a rather specious form of reasoning. 'No man,' said one, 'is so fit to take that voyage upon him as Your Grace.' 'He that achieved victory in Norfolk once already,' another added, 'is so feared that none durst once uplift their weapon against him – besides, you are the best man of war in the realm.' 'By experience, knowledge and wisdom,' another went on, 'you can animate your army with witty persuasions, and also pacify and allay your enemies' pride with your stout courage, or else dissuade them, if need were, from their enterprise.'

Northumberland continued to resist. He would not go. They abandoned persuasion and fell back on Lady Jane's commands. 'Finally,' said one, 'this is the short and the long – the Queen will in no wise grant that her father should take it on him.' 'Wherefore we think it good, if it may please Your Grace,' said a more placatory voice, 'that it lieth in you to remedy the matter.'[9]

There was a short silence. Then the Duke said, 'Well! Since ye think it good, I and mine' – he meant his sons – 'will go, not doubting of your fidelity to the Queen's Majesty, which now I leave in your custody.'[10]

He knew how desperate his situation was. But he had not yet done with the Council; they were commanded to attend him presently. Then, having chosen his subordinates and given them their orders, he went to his daughter-in-law and told her – it must have been a bitter moment – that she was to be obeyed. She thanked him 'humbly' – that is, in the approved form – adding, 'I pray you, use your diligence.' 'I will do what in me lies,' he replied.[11] As his commission was not yet made out, it was agreed that he should receive it before his departure the next day. It was now night. Northumberland returned to the Lords.

ii

By this time messengers were coming in from Norfolk and several other counties. The Earls of Bath, Mordaunt and Wharton had sent their sons and tenants to join the Princess. Lord Derby had proclaimed her in Cheshire; and in Devonshire, that stronghold of Protestantism, she had been acknowledged by Sir Peter Carew, who was to rise against her five months later. On the morning of the 12th – at the very moment that Northumberland was arguing with the Lords – the outspoken Mr Troughton of West Witham visited the aldermen of Stamford in order to persuade them to declare for the Lady Mary, but without success. Meanwhile Lord Robert Dudley had proclaimed Lady Jane at King's Lynn (where he held lands through his father-in-law, Sir John Robsart) before returning to London. Coventry, Shrewsbury, York, Stamford and Royston remained neutral, waiting on events.[12]

This news was followed by that of the first desertions in the Council's immediate circle. Sir Edward Hastings declared for the old faith he had disputed with Huntingdon in their army days, and summoned his Buckinghamshire tenants to support the Princess. Then it was discovered that Sir Edmund Peckham, cofferer to the Household, had left the Tower with some of the royal treasure.[13]

Early the next morning Northumberland collected his forces at Durham House. Having arranged for a supplementary retinue to follow him to Newmarket – for he hoped to capture the Princess Mary between there and Bury St Edmunds – he buckled on his armour, returned to the Tower and summoned the Lords. 'He was not forward,' says a contemporary, 'to take on the enterprise, being jealous of the fidelity of the Council to him, and that, during his absence, they would more easily be wrought upon to deliver up the Queen.'[14]

His heart was heavy within him. Yet he still relied on the force of his personality, on his eloquence and on his power to terrorize. Standing there in the Council Chamber, with his four tall sons, Warwick, Ambrose, Henry and Robert, beside him (Guilford, as titular King Consort, was to remain in the Tower) he appealed to the Lords for the last time in the magnificent rhetoric of his day.

'My lords,' he began, 'I and these other noble personages with the whole army, that now go forth as well for the behalf of you and yours, as for the estate and risking of the Queen's Highness, shall not only adventure our lives amongst our adversaries in the open fields, but so we do leave the conservations of ourselves, children and families at home here with you, as altogether committed to your truth and fidelities whom, if we thought ye would, through malice, conspiracy or dissension, leave us, your friends, in the briars and betray us, we could as well sundry ways foresee and provide for our own safeguards as any of you, by betraying us, can do for yours.'[15]

Then came a sudden change of tone – and a strangely protective reference to the daughter-in-law whose commands might be sending him to his death. 'But now,' he went on, 'upon the only trust and faithfulness of your honours – whereof we think ourselves most assured – we do hazard our lives, which trust and promise, if ye do violate, hoping thereby of life and promotion, yet shall not God count you innocent of our bloods, neither acquit you of the sacred and holy oath of allegiance, made freely by you, to this virtuous lady the Queen's Highness, *who, by your and our enticement, is rather by force placed thereon than by her own seeking and request.*' He then cited the

Protestant cause, the Council's promises and their signatures to the late King's will.

'Think not,' he continued, '. . . but if you mean deceit . . . thereafter God will [not] revenge the same. I can say no more, but in this troublesome time, wish you to use constant hearts, abandoning all malice, envy and private affections.'

In the pause that followed the Duke seemed to consider. Then he said, 'I have not spoken to you upon this sort upon any distrust I have of your truths, of which always I have hitherto conceived a trusty confidence; but I have put you in remembrance thereof, what chance of variance soever might grow amongst you in my absence; and this I pray you, wish me not worse good speed in this journey than you would have to yourselves.'

One of the Lords – perhaps Winchester, the eldest – replied, 'My lord, if you distrust any of us in this matter, Your Grace is far deceived – for which of us can wash his hands clear thereof? Herein your doubt is too far cast.'[16]

Northumberland was about to reply when the servants came in with the first course of the midday meal. He said resignedly, 'I pray God it be so – let us go to dinner,' and they ate together for the last time.[17]

Then with his sons, Northampton, Huntingdon, Sir John Gates and Sir Thomas Palmer, he went to receive his commission from Lady Jane. After a brief and formal leave-taking, they parted – never to meet again.

As he left the royal apartments Northumberland came upon Arundel with the page, Thomas Lovell, in the antechamber. Lovell was the Duke's body-servant: but it had been agreed that he should stay with Arundel. The two men – soon to be betrayer and betrayed – shook hands. Arundel said, 'I am sorry not to go with Your Grace. I could spend my blood even at your feet.' The Duke did not answer. He took young Lovell's hand, saying, 'Farewell, gentle Thomas, with all my heart,' and turned away.[18] As he left the Tower he said fiercely, 'In a few days I will bring in the Lady Mary, captive or dead, like a rebel as she is.'[19]

Northumberland and his companions then took barge to

Durham Place, where they mustered their men – 3,000 foot, 2,000 horse and a great train of artillery. Next day, the 14th, and the fifth of Jane's reign, they left via Shoreditch. Crowds came out to see them go. The Duke, in his scarlet cloak, riding between Warwick and Lord Grey of Wilton, said bitterly, 'Do you see, my lord, what a conflux of people here is drawn together, to see us march? And yet of all this multitude, not one wisheth us God-speed.'[20]

Grey made no answer. They were leading a highly trained, splendidly armed force – would it stand against the hatred of a nation?

NOTES

1. Pollini, *Historia Ecclesiastica*, pp 260–97.
2. Chapman, *Two Tudor Portraits*, p 169.
3. Holinshed, *Chronicle*, vol III, pp 1066–71.
4. Collins, *Letters and Memorials of State*, p 6.
5. Pollini, pp 260–97.
6. De Guaras, *The Accession of Queen Mary*, p 91.
7. Ellis, *Original Letters Illustrative of English History*, ser 3, vol III, pp 311–12.
8. *Queen Jane and Queen Mary*, ed Nichols, pp 5–6; Holinshed, vol III, pp 1068–9.
9. Ibid.
10. Ibid.
11. Ibid.
12. *Queen Jane and Queen Mary*, pp 111–13.
13. Ibid.
14. Collins, pp 22–7.
15. Ibid.
16. Ibid.
17. Holinshed, vol III, pp 1068–9.
18. Ibid.
19. De Guaras, p 91.
20. Godwin, *Annals of England*, p 264.

Chapter 3

The Struggle

THE effect of Lady Jane's decision on Northumberland's plot was fatal. Though he was a more experienced and efficient soldier than Suffolk, the situation in East Anglia did not call for skilled generalship so much as for the appearance of a popular leader, one whose Protestantism would outweigh the claims of a Catholic heiress. Furthermore, the sudden cessation of Northumberland's personal magnetism enabled the Lords to reconsider, and so to break out of the spellbound existence in which they had moved – some very unwillingly – since signing the King's devise. Each one began to look for allies elsewhere and to plan how best to play a double game, while sheltering behind the façade of Lady Jane's sovereignty. Their first step was to find out how they stood in relation to France and Spain.

They therefore sent a letter to Charles V announcing that 'the baser sort of people' had to be 'kept in order . . . Therefore . . . the Duke of Northumberland's Grace, accompanied with the Lord Marquess of Northampton, proceedeth with a convenient power into the parties of Norfolk to keep those countries in stay and obedience.' They concluded by warning the Emperor not to meddle, 'directly or indirectly', nor to 'give occasion of unkindness' to Queen Jane.[1]

Lord Cobham and Sir John Mason then interviewed Renard and de Scheyve at Baynard's Castle on Northumberland's behalf, opening the conversation in the belligerent and threatening style he generally used towards themselves. The Spanish Ambassadors' report shows that though they were not prepared to support Mary, they had begun to perceive the precariousness of the Duke's situation.

De Scheyve and Renard were not intimidated by this pair of heretical barbarians: but they were afraid of England selling out to France. When they were told that their embassy would be concluded if they continued to communicate with the Lady Mary, they made no reply. 'You well know,' Cobham went on, 'what offices are permitted to Ambassadors. The laws of England are very strict.' Mason added that if Their Excellencies fell into danger through some indiscretion, the Council would have to take action – 'and that,' he remarked significantly, 'would grieve us'.[2]

The Spaniards replied with a long list of injuries. Why had they been ignored, denied audiences and passed over for MM de Noailles and du Boisdaulphin? Renard then proceeded to lecture Cobham and Mason on the 'private ambition and greed' of the Council. 'As to our mission being at an end,' he continued haughtily, 'your lordships have no need to instruct us on that point. His Imperial Majesty hath not chosen us from among persons entirely ignorant of the powers and privileges of Ambassadors.' He then reverted to French intrigues, recalled Henry VIII's command that the Lady Mary should succeed, and concluded, 'The bare truth of the matter is that her crown hath been snatched for the Queen of Scotland under cover of conferring it upon the Duke of Suffolk's daughter.' Before the Councillors could reply, he announced his intention of leaving the country as soon as an escort could be provided.[3]

This unexpected retort alarmed Cobham and Mason. 'You are mistaken – do not yet depart – we will report your words to the Council,' they said, apparently speaking together. 'We know very well what your lordships mean by danger, and why you say it,' said Renard, adding that his master was in fact entirely devoted to English interests. 'Cobham and Mason,' he told the Emperor, 'were astonished and confused. They knew not what to answer, but sat staring at one another.' After again begging the Spaniards not to depart and paying them many compliments, 'they left us,' he concluded, 'in suspense.'[4]

Meanwhile de Noailles was imploring the rest of the Council to give the Spanish envoys their passports and send them packing. He hinted that in return Henri II would do whatever was necessary to support Queen Jane.[5] As soon as they realized this, Renard and de Scheyve asked for another audience with the Council, during which they dwelt at length on the Emperor's 'affection for England'. The Lords replied in the same strain, while making it clear that the Lady Mary's cause was doomed. This was confirmed by her messenger, who arrived at the embassy a few hours later. Her Grace's hope, he said, lay in the Emperor: for her army was less than half the size of Northumberland's and poorly armed.[6] The Spanish envoys' fear of a French alliance was now somewhat lessened; but the alternative to Henri II 'snatching' the crown for Mary Stuart was, in their view, almost as bad. 'The Duke's ambition,' wrote Renard, 'is . . . to seize the crown and hold it . . . in the person of his son . . . Our presence,' he concluded, 'can be of no profit, for every time the Council send to us, they speak only in the name of the new Queen.'[7] This resulted in Charles V telling the English Ambassador that he 'rejoiced' in the accession of Lady Jane and her husband.[8] And so, on the 14th, the day that Northumberland left London to bring Mary in, the Spaniards decided to abandon her.

The effect on Lady Jane of Franco-Spanish agitation and subservience[9] and of her own importance in European politics was shown by her taking an active, if limited, part in the administration of the kingdom. Now it was she who gave the orders, while her father and Winchester, to whom Northumberland had delegated his powers, did little or nothing. Her first action was to write to the Duke of Norfolk, who had been a prisoner in the Tower during the whole of Edward's reign, requiring him, as Earl Marshal of England, to support her, and promising to reinstate him if he did so. Norfolk, who had escaped the block by a hair's breadth in 1547, made no reply.[10] Jane then appointed a new Sheriff of Wiltshire and sent instructions to Ridley about his next sermon.

Although she had refused the crown and then accepted it in alarm and misgiving, the fact that she had accepted it now became the mainspring of her activities, such as they were. Her upbringing and temperament had produced a single-mindedness which resulted in her fulfilling her duties as a queen and a Protestant, while taking no steps about future plans. She was completely unaware of, and would not have been interested in, the general feeling about Mary and herself. Popularity with the people was something she had never thought about, partly perhaps, because she never had it. The fact that the majority of Protestants were ready to support Mary because they hated Northumberland and felt the Princess' claim to be just, was concealed from Lady Jane for the first six or seven days of her reign. At no moment was she in touch with the public – not even when she spoke to a few of them from the scaffold; nor would it ever have occurred to her that she would do well to be so. Thus, if Northumberland had succeeded in establishing her, the result would have been disastrous. Occupied in forcing ultra-Protestantism on the nation, she would have antagonized all those – a large majority – who still cared, if only in a luke-warm, sentimental manner, for the old faith. Ironically enough, it was Mary who, through a similar fanaticism, helped to bring the English people to that spiritual and doctrinal compromise so suited to the national temperament and so subtly developed by the genius of her great successor.

ii

The ruler who was eventually forced to destroy Lady Jane and her husband had now reached her thirty-eighth year. Mary had some of the qualities but little of the intellectual power which characterized the Tudors. Short, spare, deep voiced, sandy-haired and overdressed, she gave the impression of being for-midable, prepotent and harsh; those who came to know her soon perceived that she was naive, emotional and impulsive. Her interests were feminine and domestic, although she had been as highly educated as the rest of her family, she rather inclined to talk about fashions, children and household matters than to discuss politics or books. As is often the case with those whose affections have been stifled or deprived, the romantic side of her nature found its outlet in her religion. By the time she and the cousin whom she so much resembled had become unwilling rivals, Mary's faith was her sole inspiration, the focal point of her existence. To sum up, she was a kind, truthful, ultra-scrupulous woman who, if she had not been born a princess, would have made an admirable, rather commonplace, wife and mother. Yet she was not stupid; and she was incapable – unfortunately – of laziness or self-seeking. She could assume dignity, if she did not possess it: and her attitude towards her calling was vocational, energetic and unselfconscious.

The crisis of July 1553 was the second, and not the greatest, in her life. Fifteen years before, she had yielded to her father's threats and betrayed, as she saw it, the faith to which she was dedicated by acknowledging his supremacy over the Church. Thereafter, to expiate that terrible sin in whatever way God and His earthly representatives directed, became her whole purpose, her only care. To lead the people she loved and who loved her, out of the wilderness of heresy was the cause for which she now prepared to risk throne, freedom, life itself. When she realized that her appeal to the Emperor had brought, and would bring, no response, it did not occur to her to turn back, or even to wait, as he advised, for the situation to change. She was Queen of England. All she had to do was to proclaim her right, and God and the English would bring her to victory. Northumberland, his misguided little daughter-in-law, his foolish son, his perfectly trained and equipped forces and his gang of time-servers would be swallowed up, as were Pharaoh's armies in the Red Sea, when she, the daughter of the greatest king who had ever reigned in England, appeared at the head of her six hundred followers.

This simple and forthright view of her position was not wildly or impetuously put into practice. She was aware, as every Tudor was always aware, of the trends in national feeling. To some degree, Protestantism had been established within her inheritance. The fact that it was mortally sinful had nothing to do with its appeal. Apart from her rights, she had certain cards to play – and she played them as her father and grandfather had played theirs in somewhat similar circumstances. Having taken refuge in a Protestant area from Northumberland's plan to kidnap and perhaps murder her, she found herself supported by heretics, the fate of whose church lands was their chief concern. When they inquired about her intentions on matters of faith, she replied then, as circumspectly and discreetly as she did later, that she would not

'constrain or compel other men's consciences, otherwise than
God shall'. God would, she knew, 'put in their hearts a persuasion of the truth' – and the truth was obvious.[11] The Shepherd
would care for His lost sheep; all she had to do was to serve
Him.

She proceeded to do so speedily and without fear. 'She
agreed,' says an embittered Protestant contemporary, 'with
such promise, as no man would have doubted that any innova-
tion of matters of religion should have followed, by her suf-
ferance or procurement, during her reign; but how soon she
forgat that promise, it shall shortly after plainly appear.'[12] The
deduction is unjust and incorrect. Mary forgot nothing, and
was incapable of conscious deceit. She trusted in God; it was
her tragedy.

iii

From the morning of the 14th to the afternoon of the 16th the
Council remained outwardly loyal to Lady Jane. On the 15th
they wrote to certain provincial sheriffs and magistrates in her
name, affirming her possession of the crown and adding that
the Duke of Northumberland had gone to suppress the Lady
Mary's rebellion.[13] The Londoners had now accepted Jane,
partly because they did not know whether Mary was advancing to the capital or not, and were less interested in supporting
her than in avoiding trouble for themselves. The streets were
full of armed men, and Northumberland's spies were believed
to be waiting to report seditious talk. This was not so. The pay
of the Duke's forces had been so long in arrears that many had
deserted and none could be spared as informers. He himself,
now approaching Ware, called for volunteers to bring in the
Lady Mary, and raised their earnings to the enormous sum of
tenpence a day.[14] All might still have gone well for him if he
and the Lords had made up their minds to trust one another.
Their not doing so resulted in his movements being constricted
by warrant; for the Council, while themselves hovering near
desertion (Arundel had already sent to warn Mary of the
Duke's approach[15]) believed that Northumberland might

declare for her if he arrived to find her in a strong enough position. On his side, Northumberland was determined that the
Lords should be committed to all his decisions, and required
their signatures before taking action.[16] The time thus spent was
of untold value to Mary; while the Duke's messengers went to
and fro her forces increased. Before he left Ware for Cambridge his slow advance, and the fact that his men had not
even set eyes on the enemy, had disheartened them; they began
to desert so rapidly that he sent to the Council for replace-
ments.[17]

This demand reached the Tower on the night of the 15th
and made the Lords very uneasy. After a conference in which
they agreed to send a 'slender answer' to the Duke's appeal,
Arundel sought out Sir William Cecil. 'I like not the air,' he
said. Cecil replied that he was already in touch with the Lady
Mary's Grace, and that he had written under an assumed
name to the Earl of Bedford, who commanded Windsor Castle,
suggesting that he should declare for her.[18] But Cecil and
Arundel knew that they were not in a position to act alone.
Before deciding to betray Northumberland, they must find out
how far Winchester and Pembroke were prepared to go. Pembroke, though negligible as a personality, was the most important member of the Council after Northumberland. His
vast estates in Wales and the west country held an army of
tenants; if he ordered them to rise for the Princess, her victory
was assured. On the other hand, his son was married to Lady
Jane's sister, and he might lose his church lands if Northumberland was defeated. Could he be approached? Eventually
Cecil decided that Winchester, Pembroke's co-equal and ally
– who had done his best to prevent the enforcement of Edward's devise – should be sounded first. Then, if he, Pembroke, Arundel and Cecil were all agreed, they might confer –
outside the Tower – with those of the Council who seemed
interested.[19]

On the morning of the 16th Northumberland reached the
outskirts of Cambridge, and was about to proceed towards
Bury St Edmunds, when news reached him from Yarmouth,
where eight ships were waiting to seize the Princess in the

event of her trying to escape overseas. The officers had gone ashore. Sir Henry Jerningham, who was raising forces on Mary's behalf, boarded the flagship and asked the sailors to declare for her. They consented. They then saw that the captains were rowing out towards them. 'Will you have our captains or no?' a mariner asked. 'Yea, marry,' Jerningham replied. 'Ye shall have them,' he was assured, 'or else we shall throw them to the bottom of the sea.' The captains, coming aboard, accepted the situation. 'We will serve Queen Mary gladly,' said their principal, and gave orders that arms and cannon should be landed and conveyed into Norfolk.[20]

Hearing of this disaster, Northumberland wrote a second time, 'somewhat sharply', for reinforcements. While he waited for them, some of his men deserted, and he advanced on Bury St Edmunds with a diminished and rebellious force. Even then, a dash into the Princess's territory might have destroyed her hopes. He dared not make it; his nerve was beginning to fail. Meanwhile Guilford, complaining that he was not sufficiently honoured, made a scene with the Council. It was arranged that he should dine alone, in state.[21]

On the day that Northumberland reached Bury St Edmunds the Council decided to make what they may have known was their last appeal for Lady Jane. This proclamation, signed by her, was read out to the people on the 16th. It reiterated the justice of her claim, censured the Lady Mary for provoking 'matter derogatory to our title and dignity royal', and called for the preservation of the Crown 'out of the dominion of strangers and Papists'.[22] It now began to dawn on some of the Lords that if Northumberland was defeated before he could communicate with them, they might find themselves prisoners in the Tower and never leave it alive. Then news came that Mary had been proclaimed in Oxford.[23]

On the night of the 16th Pembroke and Winchester left the Tower, separately, without telling one another, for their respective houses. When Lady Jane realized this, she sent soldiers to fetch them back, and as soon as they returned, gave orders that all the gates were to be locked and the keys brought up to her by seven o'clock every night.[24] On the morning of the 17th, while

Northumberland was retreating from Bury St Edmunds to Cambridge, Renard and de Scheyve sent off their report to the Emperor.

Their last courier had been arrested by the Council: but this messenger would, they thought, be allowed to get through, because he came 'on behalf of the new Queen to impart to Your Majesty the reasons that moved the late King to nominate her as his successor', and to find out whether the Emperor was prepared to help the Lady Mary – which they advised him not to do. 'The decisive moment seems to be near,' they continued. 'In four or six days we shall hear whether people are rising.' There was a very faint chance that Mary might triumph, but 'this is doubtful and uncertain'. The Council, their spies informed them, were afraid that the Commons might not accept Lady Jane, and the guards round the Tower had been doubled in the event of a rising against her – 'for they know that the Lady Mary is loved throughout the kingdom, and that the people are aware of their wicked complaisance in allowing the Duke to cheat her of her right.' The Ambassadors had now decided to stay on. 'Before we arrive at Dover the Duke of Northumberland's expedition will have been put to the test.'[25]

By the time Charles V received this dispatch Northumberland was in Cambridge, and the Lords had left the Tower. On the morning of the 18th they met at Baynard's Castle.

NOTES

1. Ellis, *Original Letters Illustrative of English History*, ser 3, vol III, pp 311–12.

2. *Cal SP Spanish*, vol XI, pp 82–96.

3. Ibid.

4. Ibid.

5. Harbison, *Rival Ambassadors at the Court of Queen Mary*, p 50.

6. *Cal SP Spanish*, vol XI, pp 82–96.

7. Ibid.

8. Strype, *Ecclesiastical Memorials*, vol III, pt 1, pp 1–8.

9. *Cal SP Spanish*, vol XI, pp 82–96.

10. Northumberland MSS, p 304.

11. *Acts of the Privy Council*, vol IV, p 17.
12. Holinshed, *Chronicle*, vol III, p 1069.
13. *Queen Jane and Queen Mary*, ed Nichols, p 208.
14. Froude, *History of England*, vol V, p 201.
15. Carte, *History of England*, vol III, p 282.
16. Collins, *Letters and Memorials of State*, pp 22–7.
17. Holinshed, vol III, p 1071.
18. Tytler, *England under the Reigns of Edward VI and Mary*, vol II, p 203.
19. Ibid.
20. *Queen Jane and Queen Mary*, p 8.
21. *Cal SP Spanish*, vol XI, p 98.
22. Losely MSS, pp 122–6.
23. *Queen Jane and Queen Mary*, p 9.
24. Ibid.
25. *Cal SP Spanish*, vol XI, pp 91–2.

Chapter 4

The Defeat

THE Lords did not have to bribe or threaten the guards to let them out of the Tower. They regained with Lady Jane's permission what they now knew to be their freedom. Although she could be firm, even dictatorial, she was not sufficiently experienced in statecraft to imagine deception on an elaborate scale. She was told that Northumberland's struggle against the Lady Mary might be prolonged and that help from outside was essential. To apply to the Spaniards was out of the question. As the French were more friendly, the Council proposed to wait on M de Noailles. When they had found out what he was prepared to do, they would return; but the business was not one for a single envoy.

As Suffolk was too deeply committed to join them, the Council told him the same tale, 'which seemed reasonable to ... a man of no great depth himself, and not like to penetrate to the bottom of a deep design; he gave way to their departure ... little conceiving that they never meant to come back.'[1] At the last moment he became suspicious, and tried to join them; they threatened him with death if he deserted his daughter, and he yielded. So Jane, Guilford, the Suffolks, the Duchess of Northumberland and their attendants remained in the state apartments, unaware that in two days they would be leaving them for the last time.

Baynard's Castle, then Pembroke's residence, where his son and Lady Katherine Grey were still awaiting his orders as to the consummation of their marriage,[2] was the most magnificent of the remaining Thames-side Gothic palaces. Set between Blackfriars and Paul's Wharf, it soared above the neighbouring structures, and was luxuriously furnished with the spoils of a hundred churches. Its inner spaciousness was enriched by such tapestries as showed 'a king riding in a chariot in a blue gown with stars: a woman in a cloud with a world in her hand ... between a fire and a city; one riding upon a white horse ... hawking and hunting scene with naked boys at the corners; a woman in childbed with some women in her chamber'. The gardens stretched to where the Bank of England now stands, and the main entrance was the water-gate, so that from that side the mansion seemed to be set in, rather than upon, the river.[3]

Here the Lords forgathered in the Council chamber, as for a formal debate. This was opened by Arundel. 'My Lords and dear brethren,' he began, and at once plunged into a furious indictment of Northumberland. He first cited the Duke's 'injuries' against them as a body; then he turned to what concerned him most. 'You remember,' he went on, 'how unjustly and unworthily he detained me in prison almost a whole year ... By the force of innocency and truth I escaped the inextricable snares of my mortal enemy.' Then followed a long description of Northumberland's monstrous treatment of Somerset, that good Duke, and Arundel's dear friend. 'What shall we determine of him,' he continued, 'who has designed to imbrue his hands, not in the blood of one or two, but utterly to destroy so many lives at one blow? ... Now we may freely speak of our sentiments ... The crown is due to Mary –' and he broke off to quote Henry VIII's will.

'What is objected against this?' Arundel pursued, now warming to his theme, as that which lay nearest the hearts of his audience. 'The cause of religion, forsooth, and the danger of a foreign husband! But for God's sake, what imprudence and blindness is it ... to cast ourselves and our fortunes precipitately upon certain ruin!' Suddenly his tone became one of fearful warning. 'Have you forgotten Dudley's arts? The most pernicious outrages are often committed in the name of religion.' He then appeared to communicate with the spirit of the great Lucifer who had tried to destroy him. 'And who told you, Dudley –' he went on – 'for I desire to address myself to you, though absent – that the Lady Mary would marry a foreign husband?' After sustaining this form of oratory for some time, he returned to the Lords in the pathetic-manly style. 'My Lords and most worshipful brethren, I implore your prudence and equity.' He begged them not to delay in supporting the Princess, and so concluded.

Arundel and Pembroke must have rehearsed with care; for as one sat down the other rose. 'My Lords,' Pembroke cried. 'I am ready to fight with any man –' he clapped his hand on his sword – 'who should proclaim the contrary. This blade shall make Mary Queen, or I will lose my life!'[4]

After some further discussion it was agreed that John Dudley, Duke of Northumberland, was a traitor to Queen Mary. His surrender was demanded and a letter requiring his submission and the dismissal of his army written and dispatched. 'If he does not obey,' was the conclusion of the debate, 'we, of all the nobility ... will ... persecute him and his, to their utter confusion.'[5] The Mayor of London was sent for, and it was then arranged that if they received no reply from Northumberland, Arundel should proceed to Cambridge to arrest the villain who had led them all astray and betrayed their honour. It was now nearly dinner-time. But first they must publicly thank God for their deliverance from Northumberland's evil toils; they set off for St Paul's, where they ordered Mass to be celebrated.

By the morning of the 19th the Lords had received no answer from Northumberland; Arundel therefore left to arrest him, going first to make his own peace with Mary. He travelled night and day, arriving at Cambridge on the 20th.[6]

Meanwhile the Council made their change of allegiance public and official by (1) sending two of their number to tell Suffolk that Lady Jane's reign was over, (2) informing the foreign Ambassadors that the Lady Mary was Queen, (3) proclaiming her in London and the provinces and, (4) sending her their loyal submission. These duties were carried out simultaneously, and the substitution of Mary for Jane was so smoothly accomplished that the thirteen days which passed between Edward's death and Mary's accession seemed a meaningless interim to those not involved in Northumberland's plot; soon the nine days' reign was thought of as an unpleasant but trivial delay to the good times which were coming with the Queen everyone loved.

The announcement of Mary's triumph left the Spanish Ambassadors in a sceptical and suspicious mood. Renard thought the English 'so treacherous, inconstant, false, malicious and easily roused, that little trust is to be placed in them.'[7] Also, he was as yet uncertain, he told the Emperor, 'of the reasons that moved these gentlemen to make their new proclamation.'[8] When the Princess was proclaimed his doubts were partially allayed by 'the greatest rejoicing it is possible to imagine, and such a concourse of people as never was seen, who came forth as if they had been waiting to hear that my Lady's right was restored to her.'[9] Bonfires and bells went on all day and all night; people danced in the streets, embracing and crying for joy.

Renard's suspicions were roused again when he and his fellows were visited at their private lodgings by an old woman, who asked them to warn the Lady Mary to beware of the Council. 'This,' Renard says, '... gave us pause, and we were unable to think in what manner they could manage to deceive her; but ... we thought we saw what they were trying to do; namely, to induce my Lady to lay down her arms, and then treacherously ... encompass her death.'[10] It may have been so; such a scheme might well be evolved by some Councillor who was still not sure that Mary would succeed.

At the same time Renard was informed that Northumberland had sent his cousin Sir Henry Dudley to France with a request for support, and that 6,000 men were being embarked from Calais and Dieppe. If this were so, the Lady Mary would almost certainly be defeated. Spain must therefore remain neutral, for if she did not, those 'violent and implacable French' might take the opportunity to advance Mary Stuart's claim – and that would be infinitely worse than the restoration of Lady Jane.[11] Renard therefore sent to advise Mary not to lay down her arms till she was certain of her position (she had no intention of doing so, and was now proceeding slowly and with the utmost caution); he assured her at the same time that her victory was a miraculous demonstration of the Divine Will.[12]

When Suffolk heard that his daughter's reign had ended, he received the news as if he had expected it all along. Finding her at supper in the state apartments, he himself tore down the canopy. Then he told her that she was no longer Queen, adding, 'You must put off your royal robes and be content with a private life.' Jane replied, 'I much more willingly put them off than I put them on. Out of obedience to you and my mother, I have grievously sinned. Now I willingly relinquish the crown.' Then she said innocently, 'May I not go home?'[13]

To this Suffolk made no answer; and indeed there could be none, for he intended to ensure his own safety by leaving her a prisoner in order to prove his loyalty to Queen Mary. If he were to get out of the Tower alive, it should be without her, and at once.

Jane then retired to the private apartments, where her ladies were awaiting her. When she told them what had happened, there were sobs and wailings. She said quietly that she was very glad she was no longer Queen.[14] For the rest of that day and those following it she remained in the 'inner room' described by a contemporary,[15] unmolested by her husband and her mother-in-law, who were in another part of the White Tower. Meanwhile her father, whom she was never to see again, came out on to Tower Hill, after commanding his men-at-arms to leave their weapons behind. 'I am but one man,' he said, 'but I here proclaim the Lady Mary's Grace Queen of England.' He then made his way to Sheen, where he was followed by the Duchess of Suffolk a few days later.[16]

ii

Before Northumberland left Bury St Edmunds his troops were fighting amongst themselves and no reinforcements had arrived to replace the many hundreds of deserters. He returned to Cambridge on the evening of the 18th determined to continue the struggle with such weapons as still lay ready to his hand; one was the subjugation of the University, that cradle of Protestantism and training-centre of the scholars whom Henry

VIII and Edward VI had delighted to honour – Cheke,
Ascham, Cranmer, and Lady Jane's tutors.

As soon as he arrived the Duke sent for the Vice-Chancellor,
Dr Sandys, and some attendant dons, and outlined their part
in the campaign. 'Masters,' he concluded, 'pray for us that we
speed well.' He added with a touch of his old jocosity, 'You
shall be made bishops, and we deacons.' (A rather grim double
meaning lay within this last remark; to be made deacon was a
slang term for decapitation.) The Duke then desired Sandys
to preach next day on behalf of Lady Jane and the Protestant
cause, and dismissed him.[17]

The Vice-Chancellor lay awake a long time, seeking inspiration for his sermon. At three in the morning it occurred to him
to drop his Bible on the floor and preach from the first text at
which it fell open. As is usually the case, this time-honoured
ruse produced a suitable theme; it was from the first chapter of
the Book of Joshua. 'All that thou commandest us we will do,
and whithersoever thou sendest us we will go. According as we
hearkened unto Moses in all things, so will we hearken unto
thee; only the Lord thy God be with thee, as he was with
Moses. Whosoever he be that doth rebel against thy commandment and will not hearken to thy words in all that thou commandest him, he shall be put to death: only be strong and of a
good courage.'[18]

Dr Sandys started work at once. He was still writing when
news came that Queen Mary was proclaimed, and that Northumberland's officers had received orders from the Council to
disperse their men 'whither they will.'[19] By this time Northumberland was in the precincts of King's. Here he was arrested by
Slegge, the University sergeant-at-arms, in the Queen's name.

Flaring up into one of his famous rages, the Duke managed
to overawe his captors. 'Ye do me wrong to withdraw my
liberty,' he shouted. 'See ye not the Council's letters, without
exception, that all men should go whither they would?'[20] He
was set free and, sending for Sandys, went out to the market-
place.

The tall, elegant figure in the scarlet cloak and the dark-clad
shape of the Vice-Chancellor were then seen making their way

to where the proclamation of Lady Jane still hung. Northumberland tore it down, and waving his white baton, shouted, 'Long live Queen Mary!' He tried to laugh – he did laugh; but the tears were running down his face.[21]

It was now time for morning service. Northumberland, his sons and his general staff, went to Great St Mary's. When Sandys ascended the pulpit the Duke called him down and told him to celebrate Mass. Dr Sandys was not so easily defeated. He had taken some trouble over his sermon, and he delivered it. Then he compromised by conducting the service according to Catholic usage. As he and the Duke left together, Northumberland said, 'Queen Mary is a merciful woman. I look for a general pardon.' 'My life is not dear to me,' the Vice-Chancellor replied. 'Neither have I said or done anything that urgeth my conscience.' Having justified his sermon, he turned to Northumberland, and went on, 'But be you assured, you shall never escape death; for if she would save you, those that now rule will kill you.'[22]

Northumberland did not answer. He returned to his lodgings and there, with Warwick, Ambrose and Henry Dudley (Lord Robert had been captured outside Bury St Edmunds) he evolved a plan of escape. They were making ready to ride – Northumberland was putting on his boots – when they heard a clatter on the stairs. The door opened. Arundel – whose last words had been, 'I could shed my blood, even at your feet' – stood before him.

There was then no need of explanation. In those few seconds, as the two men faced one another, Northumberland's defences collapsed. His sons, standing behind him, saw their magnificent father change into a cringing suppliant. Before Arundel could speak, the Duke fell on his knees. 'Be good to me, for the love of God,' he said, 'and consider – I have done nothing but by the consents of you all, and the whole Council.' Arundel replied. 'My lord, I am sent hither by the Queen's Majesty, and in her name I do arrest you.' 'And I obey it, my lord,' the Duke assured him, 'and I beseech you, my lord of Arundel, use mercy towards me, knowing the case as it is.' 'My lord,' said Arundel coldly, 'ye should have sought for mercy sooner. I must do according to my commandment.'[23] He then put Northumberland in charge of the guards who had come with him, and arrested his sons and his general staff.

Northumberland was allowed to address his sad captains; in a last attempt to assert himself, he declared in a loud voice, 'All I have done up to this time hath been enacted with the knowledge, authority and consent of the Council, in proof of which I have documents sealed with the Great Seal of England. But I wish not to combat the Council's decisions, supposing that they have been moved by good reasons and considerations, and I beg your lordships to do the same.'[24]

The Mayor of Cambridge then arrived to take him into custody. As the Duke gave up his sword he said, 'I am subject to the law, and desire to obey the law.' He looked round for his servants; they had fled, tearing the badge of the bear and the ragged staff from their caps as they ran.[25]

He was locked up in the outer room of his lodgings and left alone. Once or twice he asked leave to go to the bedchamber; this was not allowed. For two hours he walked up and down. Then, looking out, he saw Arundel, that free and faithful servant of the Queen, crossing the courtyard. Before the guards could stop him he opened the window and called, 'My lord of Arundel – my lord! I pray a word with you.' 'What would you have, my lord?' 'I beseech your lordship,' said the Duke, 'for the love of God, let me have Cox, one of my chamber, to wait on me.' 'You shall have Tom, your boy,' said Arundel after a moment's consideration. 'Alas! my lord,' Northumberland pleaded, 'what stead can a boy do me? I pray you let me have Cox.' Arundel graciously sent him both Thomas Lovell and Cox.[26] After all, it was not fitting that the man who had ruled England should remain unattended. And besides, he could be humiliated in other ways.

While Arundel awaited instructions from Queen Mary, who was now at Newhall, Northumberland and his fellow-prisoners remained in Cambridge. They left on the 24th, reaching London at dusk the next day. Arundel rode beside the Duke and his sons; Gates, Palmer and Northampton followed under a separate escort.

This was Arundel's triumph; and crowds lined the streets to share it with him. From the moment they entered the city Northumberland's escort had to be doubled; even then he was in danger of being lynched. The guards struck at the people with their pikes: the frightened horses reared and plunged; but no injury, no violence could hold back the furious and ecstatic mob. They threw stones, rotten eggs, filth from the gutters; they rushed upon the horsemen, trying to get at the figure in the scarlet cloak and yelling, 'Death! Death to the traitor!' Four eyewitnesses – the Greyfriars chronicler, a Spanish merchant, Renard and Father Perlin – have left an account of the scene.

'Before them,' says the Ambassador, 'rode four ensigns, leading a force of cavalry, archers and men-at-arms, all mounted and equipped in the English fashion ... Armed men were posted all along the streets, to prevent the people, greatly excited as they were, from falling upon the Duke.' At first, Perlin noted, Northumberland maintained a contemptuous hauteur, glaring back at the crowds. Arundel, observing this, decided to humble him further; as they reached Bishopsgate he told the Duke to take off his hat – and thereafter, according to Renard, 'it was always in his hand.' At Shoreditch the situation became really dangerous; but, 'for all they were spoken to', says the Greyfriars chronicler, the people went on trying to break through; the noise was appalling. At Temple Bar, Arundel, fearing that his prisoner might be snatched from him, desired Northumberland to remove his cloak. It was useless. They knew him, haggard, degraded, bedraggled though he was. 'He wished,' Renard thought, 'to move the people and his friends to pity; but notwithstanding his courtesy, the people cried out upon him. A dreadful sight ... a strange mutation.'

Bowing, bare-headed, splashed and stained, the Duke kept something of his old arrogance. Throughout that slow, hideous progress he neither flinched nor trembled. It was too much for his eldest son; as they reached the Tower, Warwick dropped the reins, covered his face and burst into tears.[27]

NOTES

1. Heylyn, *History of the Reformation*, p 163.
2. Chapman, *Two Tudor Portraits*.
3. Howard, *Life of Lady Jane Grey*, p 194.
4. De Thou, *History of His Own Time*, pp 602–3.
5. Collins, *Letters and Memorials of State*, pp 22–7.
6. *Queen Jane and Queen Mary*, ed Nichols, p 10.
7. *Cal SP Spanish*, vol XI, p 431.
8. Ibid, p 96.
9. Ibid.
10. Ibid.
11. Ibid, p 104.
12. Ibid, p 105.
13. Baker, *Chronicle*, p 90; Godwin, *Annals of England*, p 271; Pollini, *Historia Ecclesiastica*.
14. De Thou, p 603.
15. Ibid.
16. *Queen Jane and Queen Mary*, p 12.
17. Foxe, *Acts and Monuments*, vol VIII, p 599.
18. Ibid.
19. Collins, pp 22–7.
20. Ibid.
21. Foxe, vol VIII, p 599.
22. Ibid.
23. *Queen Jane and Queen Mary*, p 10.
24. *Cal SP Spanish*, vol XI, pp 111–17.
25. Ibid.
26. *Queen Jane and Queen Mary*, p 11.
27. *Antiquarian Repertory*, vol IV, p 504; *Cal SP Spanish*, vol XI, p 119; de Guaras, *The Accession of Queen Mary*, p 97; Holinshed, *Chronicle*, vol IV, p 3; *Greyfriars Chronicle*, ed Nichols, pp 78–81.

Part IV

The Final Deliverance

> Yet do I assuredly trust that this my offence towards
> God is so much the less, in that being in so royal estate
> as I was, my enforced honour never mingled with mine
> innocent heart.
>
> Lady Jane Grey to the Duke of Suffolk

Chapter 1

The Triumph of Queen Mary

N o w that Mary's accession was assured, the Spanish Ambassador referred to Lady Jane as 'her who calls herself Queen', or 'Jane of Suffolk'. The Emperor replied with remarks about 'the pretended Queen', adding that he had always known the English would be 'led by affection' to Queen Mary.[1]

In the eleven days that elapsed between Northumberland's capture and Mary's state entry into London, Jane's suite was reduced to four persons – Nurse Ellen, Mrs Tilney, Lady Throckmorton (Sir Nicholas' wife) and a page. With them, she left the White Tower for the Gentleman-Gaoler's lodgings on the Green. Guilford was removed to the Beauchamp Tower, where he was joined by his father and his four brothers (Lord Robert arrived from the prisoners' camp on the 27th), Northampton, Gates and Palmer. One of their warders was that Edward Underhill patronized by Huntingdon when he was in command at Calais. On the last day of Lady Jane's reign Mrs Underhill gave birth to a son, and her husband asked Jane to stand godmother. She consented, and the child was to be named Guilford; but by the time the christening took place, she was no longer allowed to leave her rooms, and sent Lady Throckmorton as proxy. A few days later Winchester, calling on her for the return of the Queen's jewels, heard of Underhill's impertinence and spoke very severely to Lady Jane for subscribing to it; as a prisoner, she had no rights.[2] He then turned to the matter of the Crown Imperial, which he required her to relinquish formally, together with everything she had received from the royal wardrobe. The list included furs, hats, buttons, velvet and sable mufflers, a helmet, garters, clocks and portraits of the Duchess of Suffolk, Henry VIII and Edward VI.[3]

Some of these may have been Lady Jane's own property; that

made no difference. Winchester went through her and Guilford's possessions, leaving them without a penny to fee their gaolers. Jane was allowed writing materials and a few books, including her Greek Testament and the minute Prayer Book bound in black velvet, now in the British Museum. It had originally been given to the Duke of Northumberland (or perhaps to Suffolk) by Guilford, who wrote in it, 'Your loving and obedient son wisheth unto Your Grace long life in this world, with as much joy and comfort as ever I wish to myself; and in the world to come joy everlasting. Your most humble son till his death G. Duddeley [sic].'[4]

Now Lady Jane was forbidden all communication with Guilford, or with her father, who had been arrested at Sheen and brought back to the Tower on July 28th. Suffolk managed to obtain an interview with Winchester in order to send an abject message to Queen Mary. He did not mention his daughter, and Winchester gave a non-committal answer to his plea for mercy. Three days later he was set free.

On the 26th the Duchess of Northumberland was released, and set off to Newhall to plead for her husband and sons. She was within five miles of the manor-house when she was told that the Queen would not receive her. Mary was then approached by the Duchess of Suffolk, to whom she gave a private audience.

Frances Suffolk wasted no time over her daughter's misdemeanours; bent on proving her own and Suffolk's innocence, she told Mary that Northumberland had tried to poison not only the late King but her husband. Asked for proof, she replied that an apothecary in Northumberland's employ had just committed suicide. She was then allowed to return to Sheen. Neither she nor Suffolk made any attempt to exculpate Jane, or to see her. She had failed; they must try to ignore her existence; and the fact that she was being ill treated – so Renard joyfully reported – could not be helped.

Lady Jane therefore set about putting her own case before the Queen. She had nothing to help her but eloquence and clearness of mind, and her burning indignation at having been used and betrayed. At the same time, she was aware that in accepting the crown, she had sinned, although not, she believed, unforgivably. She decided to fight for her life, and did so in a long letter which Mary received shortly after she took up residence in the White Tower on August 5th.

This document, which describes in detail Jane's feelings and actions from the afternoon of her arrival at Sion House to that when she refused to make Guilford king, is lengthy but succinct, and dignified even in its self-accusations. Jane made no claim on her relationship with the Queen or on their former intimacy. 'Although my fault be such,' she begins, 'that, but for the goodness and clemency of the Queen, I can have no hope of pardon nor in finding forgiveness, having given ear to those who at that time appeared ... to be wise, and have now shown themselves to be the contrary, having with such shameful boldness tried to give to others that which was not theirs ... (wherefore ... am I ashamed to ask pardon for such a crime) nevertheless I trust in God, that as I now know and confess my want of prudence ... I can still ... conceive hope of your infinite clemency, it being known that the error imputed to me hath not been altogether caused by myself. For whereas I might take upon me that of which I was not worthy, yet no one can ever say either that I sought it ... or that I was pleased with it.' Then follows an account of the scenes at Suffolk Place, Sion House and the White Tower. She concludes, 'The Duke was the first to persuade King Edward to make me his heir ... I know for certain that twice during this time poison was given to me.' She describes her symptoms and adds, 'All these things I have wished to say, for the witness of my innocence and the disburdening my conscience.'[5]

While Lady Jane was composing this statement the rejoicings at her defeat continued, and some of those who had helped to make her the prisoner of the State established themselves under the new régime. Her father and mother remained in discreet retirement at Sheen. Arundel took over the administration of the Council and Pembroke (who had made a good impression by throwing a capful of money to the crowds outside Baynard's Castle) began the dissolution of the thirteen-year-old Katherine Grey's marriage to his son by turning her out of the house.[6] The bonfires, 'shouting and crying of people, ringing of bells ... banqueting and singing in the streets'[7] reached their climax when Mary, looking, Renard thought, 'more than middling fair' and dressed in violet velvet,[8] rode into her capital and entered the Tower. Here she began what promised to be a reign of mercy by releasing those imprisoned before and during her brother's reign – the Duchess of Somerset, the Duke of Norfolk, Bishop Gardiner, and young Lord Courtenay, 'the last sprig of the White Rose'.[9] This youth, the great-grandson of Edward IV, and son of the Marquess of Exeter executed by Henry VIII, had a claim to the throne which nearly cost him his life when Northumberland proclaimed Lady Jane; fifteen of his twenty-five years had been spent in captivity. These persons were kneeling in the courtyard of the White Tower when Mary arrived; she kissed them and said smiling, 'These are *my* prisoners.' They were then set free.[10]

Next day a curious scene took place between the Queen and those Lords of the Council who were not in prison and who, less than a fortnight ago, had proclaimed her a bastard and a rebel. They now assured her of their unshakeable loyalty; though all had been as deeply implicated in Northumberland's conspiracy as himself (their signatures to Edward's will were there to prove it), she could not imprison them; if she had, there would have been no Council and no one to conduct the Government. She therefore compromised with a general reproof and refused to pardon them at once; but she allowed them to kiss her hand. Some wept; all abased themselves; then they resumed their duties.[11]

Mary now turned to Simon Renard as the only person she could trust, and he at once acquired a permanent and fatal ascendancy over her. They began by discussing the question of her marriage with the Emperor, from whom she had already received a long letter of advice as to the lenient treatment of the rebels (a general massacre would be a great mistake) and tactful methods with heretics. It would be inadvisable, her Imperial cousin considered, to have Mass said at the late King's obsequies, as she proposed. The people would object; and as Edward had died outside the communion of the Church, he was damned in any case.[12] Mary was obstinate. Edward should be buried in the Abbey according to Protestant rites; but she herself would attend a requiem Mass sung for him in the Tower.

She then told Renard that she did not wish to marry an Englishman; 'and indeed,' the Ambassador wrote, 'there is no match for her in England, unless it be ... Courtenay, who is of the blood royal.' If His Majesty did not wish to wed her himself – and at his age that might be too much of an undertaking – would not 'our Prince' (later Philip II) be a suitable husband?[13]

A few days later Mary saw Renard alone in order to discuss the Emperor's letter. 'His Majesty,' she said, 'hath advised mercy. Is it his wish that I should pardon the Duke of Northumberland?' She added that as she had not pardoned anybody yet, she was still free to do so.

Renard was horrified. He restrained an outburst of protest, and replied that Her Grace had completely misunderstood his master's meaning. 'Your Majesty,' he said, 'should not spare the Duke – nor those others –' he added – 'who were his closest adherents.' He mentioned the Marquess of Northampton as especially worthy of death, and remarked, 'He is generally held to be the guiltiest, after Northumberland, and his trial and execution should take place as soon as possible.'[14]

Mary seemed to agree to this, and Renard passed on to 'Jane of Suffolk', who also should be tried and condemned, with her husband.

By now Mary had had time to consider Jane's letter. She utterly refused to allow such a reprisal. 'I will not consent that she should die,' she exclaimed. 'Three days before they went to fetch her from Sion House to the Tower and make her entry as usurping Queen, she knew nothing of it, nor was she ever a party, nor did she ever give her consent to the Duke's intrigues and plots. My conscience,' she went on, 'will not permit me to have her put to death.' Renard said something about Lady Jane's marriage. 'There can have been none,' the Queen replied, 'between her and Guilford, as she was previously betrothed.'

Renard was not going to abandon the plan he afterwards described as 'the obliteration of the whole house of Suffolk' so easily; he reverted to Northumberland. There could be no question of his being pardoned, he said, and at length Mary agreed. Then he again raised the matter of Jane's death. Mary would not hear of it. At fifteen, the little cousin to whom she had given presents – and of whom, in spite of her heresy, she had been very fond – could not be considered responsible, and was therefore guiltless. Renard searched for a suitable precedent, and then said, 'The Emperor Theodosius caused Maximus, his son, to be put to death, notwithstanding his tender age, because Maximus arbitrarily attributed to himself the title of Emperor, with the intention of transmitting it to his son. History relates that the son was put to death because of the scandal and danger that might have followed ...' He went on: 'The title she hath borne, though in itself insufficiently proved, yet hath some semblance of foundation, and this might be revived again to trouble the succession of the crown. Power and tyranny have sometimes more force, especially in affairs of State, than right or justice.'[15]

Mary made no reply, and Renard went on to warn her against the Princess Elizabeth, whom he described as clever, ambitious and sly, urged Pembroke's trial and execution and again reverted to Lady Jane, imploring Her Majesty to exercise the utmost caution with regard to this dangerous young person. He finally extracted a promise that she should remain in prison for the present.[16] The Ambassador and the Queen concluded their talk with a long discussion on the religious question, with the result that Mary's intentions were given to the public in her 'pronouncement' of August 8th.

Mary began by declaring that, while herself adhering to the faith in which she had been brought up, she 'minded not to compel' her people to follow her example; she 'would be glad' merely, if they were reconciled to Catholicism. She begged them not to use 'these new-found, devilish terms of Papist or heretic', warned them against individual interpretations of Scripture, and only forbade them to preach without licence, to compose and circulate blasphemous literature and to resuscitate Northumberland's rebellion against herself. Rather naively, she ended by commanding 'her good and loving subjects to live together in Christian charity', thus depriving them of their favourite pursuit, that of acrimonious and abusive debate on matters of doctrine.[17]

The contrast between Lady Jane's and Queen Mary's respective attitudes towards religious dissension is interesting. Within a few weeks of the Queen's issuing her statement (in which she was careful not to condemn or even to find fault with, the reformed faith) Jane was composing one of her own, in the form of a letter. In this she described the Catholics as Romish anti-Christians, their Church as the Whore of Babylon and desired her correspondent to turn from 'the most wicked Mass' and 'the swill of strangers, to the delicates of your most benign and loving Father'.[18]

This and other examples of Lady Jane's views were reported to the Queen. She would not be shaken. Jane and Guilford must stand their trial; it followed that they would be found guilty and 'cast', according to the current phrase. Meanwhile they were given the Queen's promise of pardon and eventual release.[19]

ii

In the days that passed between the funeral of Edward VI and Northumberland's attainder it was rumoured that from beneath the altar in the chapel of Henry VII the young King's voice had been heard, 'crying out for vengeance' on the wicked Duke.[20] Northumberland began his captivity calmly, setting about his defence with the confidence of a man whose judges were self-condemned; this was why he asked that he should be tried by his peers. He was given three weeks to prepare his case. It was then reported to Mary that he had planned her assassination and begun negotiations for the sale of Calais and Boulogne to Henri II through Sir Henry Dudley, who was extradited to bear witness against him. Dudley got himself out of trouble by laying all the blame on the King of France, who, he said, had offered to support Lady Jane with a fleet and an army.[21] Meanwhile, the Londoners, enraged by Mass being celebrated in St Paul's – during a fearful uproar one of the congregation threw a dagger at the priest – were beginning to say that they would rather see Northumberland freed than change their religion. The Lords started to complain — why had not Her Majesty rewarded them for their change of front? — and a movement was inaugurated to marry Courtenay to the Queen. Charles V, hearing of these distressing outbreaks, attributed them to the sinister influence of Lady Jane, and wrote to Mary begging her to 'keep Jane of Suffolk in some place safe where she can be watched … so that there is no fear of her troubling the kingdom'. Renard supplemented this advice by imploring her to marry a Spaniard; he was too tactful to mention Prince Philip at this juncture: but his name was in both their minds. The Prince, hearing what was expected of him, told Charles V that as an obedient son he would be willing to marry the Queen of England (whom he referred to as his aunt) if desired to do so.[22]

There could be no question of the Queen's marrying till after her coronation; and this must be preceded by the settlement of her account with the principal rebels. Northumberland, Warwick and Northampton were summoned to appear at Westminster Hall on August 18th: Gates, Palmer, Sir Andrew Dudley (Northumberland's brother), Henry, Ambrose and Robert Dudley on the following day. As was then the custom, the trials were formal and the verdict was predetermined. All would be condemned; but it was already decided that only Northumberland, Gates and Palmer should suffer the extreme penalty. Guilford's trial was postponed, so that he might appear with Lady Jane.

In such a case, the prisoners' defence, as the word is now understood, was practically non-existent. They were allowed to call two witnesses to speak for them; on this occasion none did so, knowing that their best plan was to acknowledge their guilt, throw themselves on the Queen's mercy and plead any extenuating circumstances that might be acceptable to their judges, who were also her advisers. Forty-eight hours was generally the longest time allowed to pass between sentence and execution, during which relatives and friends could intrigue or beg for remittal, in the hope that the decision made before the hearing would be changed.

When he left the Beauchamp Tower for Westminster Hall, Northumberland had three lines of escape: the bribery or intimidation of his judges, the Queen's known disinclination to begin her reign with bloodshed and her desire to convert highly placed persons. His principal judge was Norfolk, whom he had kept in prison for six years; the others, his former allies, were bent on reinstating themselves at his expense. Thus his best chance lay in asking for postponement of execution for the purposes of spiritual enlightenment.

The trial of the man who had been dictator of England and a European power was a great event. So that the setting should be worthy of the occasion, Westminster Hall was redecorated with fresh tapestries and carpets; the judges' seats had new canopies and cushions.[23] Norfolk, now in his eighties, represented the Queen as Earl Marshal of England, sitting above the rest in a chair adorned with a pall and the royal arms. Winchester sat on his right, Bedford on his left. Below these were twenty-five Lords of the Council, all of whom had signed Edward's devise. On either side were four aldermen representing the City of London and four lawyers in white and scarlet hoods. Behind them stood the heralds and officers of the Court. Those members of the public who had bribed or forced their way in stood at the back of the Hall.[24]

When the judges had taken their places and Norfolk had touched the white wand of office held towards him by the Sheriff, a herald called for silence, and their commission was read out in Latin. Then the herald shouted, 'John Dudley, Duke of Northumberland, come into the Court!'

First came the headsman carrying the axe, its edge turned away from the prisoner, who appeared under escort. (Rather less than two years ago he had sat in Norfolk's place, facing Somerset.) He bowed low to the judges, receiving a cool nod in reply. The Recorder of London then read out his deposition – a full confession of his crimes – and went on, 'John Dudley, Duke of Northumberland, hold up thy hand. Dost thou acknowledge all that is herein stated, so that judgement may be given according to custom?' The Duke raised his right hand. 'I do,' he replied.

The Court now settled down to listen to an abject harangue, followed by the usual plea for mercy. Northumberland said, 'My lords – I would have your lordships' opinion on two points. Whether a man doing any act by authority of the Prince and Council, and by warrant of the Great Seal of England, *and doing nothing without the same,* may be charged with treason for anything he might do by warrant thereof? And secondly, whether any such persons as are equally culpable in that crime – those by whose letters and commandment he was directed in all his doings – may be his judges, or pass upon his trial as his peers?'

There seems to have been no sign of surprise or embarrassment at this defiance of precedent. Norfolk replied, 'The Great Seal which you laid for your warrant was not the lawful seal of the realm, but of an usurper, and therefore could be no warrant unto you. As to your second question, if any are to be as deeply touched in this case as yourself, yet so long as no attainder is of record against them, they are able in law to pass on any trial, and not to be challenged therefore, save at the Prince's pleasure.'[25]

Northumberland having, as he believed, one more card to play, behaved with dignity. He knelt and confessed the indictment. Sentence of hanging, drawing and quartering was passed; slowly the edge of the axe turned towards him. He stood up and said, 'I beseech you, my lords all, to be humble suitors to the Queen's Majesty to grant me four requests.' These were that he should be beheaded, that the Queen would not revenge herself on his children, that he might see a priest and that he might be allowed to speak privately with two of the Council.[26]

His appeal was noted and Warwick and Northampton were called to the bar. Warwick refused to plead, merely asking that his wife and children should not be penalized. Northampton said that he had not signed Edward's will till after his death, and then under pressure from Northumberland. He cried, and begged for mercy.[27]

Then the Duke of Norfolk rose, and breaking his white staff, declared the Court dismissed. The prisoners returned to the

Tower. The other ring-leaders were condemned the next day, which was spent by Northumberland in being reconciled to the Catholic faith. He sent for Bishop Gardiner, and said, 'I would do penance all the days of my life, if it were but in a mouse-hole – is there no hope of mercy?' 'Your offence is great,' Gardiner replied, 'and you would do well to provide for the worst – especially to see that you stand well with God in matters of conscience and religion; for to speak plainly, I think that you must die.' The Duke began to weep. 'I can be of no other faith but yours,' he said. 'I never was of any other, indeed. I complied in King Edward's days only out of ambition, for which I pray God to forgive me – and I promise I will declare that at my death.'[28]

His condition was so pitiable that Gardiner wept with him, leaving to plead for his life with the Queen. Mary hesitated; within a few hours Renard obtained a private audience, and she signed the warrant.[29] The Lieutenant of the Tower was then instructed to proceed, and the scaffold was put up on Tower Hill. The Duke, having heard that he must die the next day, wrote to Arundel. 'Alas, my good lord,' he began, 'is my crime so heinous? . . . A living dog is better than a dead lion. Oh, if it would please her good Grace to give me life, yea, but the life of a dog, if I might but live and kiss her feet . . . How little profit my dead and dismembered body can bring her . . . Spare not, I pray, your bended knees for me in this distress . . . Oh, good my lord, remember how sweet life is, and how bitter the contrary . . . God grant me patience to endure and a heart to forgive the whole world. Once your fellow and loving companion . . . John Dudley.'[30]

This appeal resulted in the postponement of execution for three days, so that the Duke might make his peace with God. A priest was sent to him, and he gave himself up to prayer.

Although his state was one of grovelling misery, Northumberland was not reduced to mindless terror; his last speeches and actions show that he knew what he was doing. His body was doomed; with characteristic thoroughness he prepared to save his soul. And so it was that the persecutor of Catholics returned to the faith in which he had been brought up; the Catholic God (he had always known it) would be merciful, provided that repentance was total, abject and sincere. The Duke's was all these; he left nothing undone and no loopholes in his submission. In fact, his reconciliation may be regarded as genuine; for he knew that he had nothing to gain by it in this world; so he would be rewarded with eventual (although delayed) entry into a kingdom peopled by those whose religion he had tried to destroy. When he was a child, a youth, the Catholic Church had supported and embraced him; now in death it resumed its power. His conversion, an excellent example of the triumph of early influences, was described as an 'ungodly and shameful end' by the Calvinists and a 'miraculous recognition' by the French Ambassador. Lady Jane, standing in the window of the Gentleman-Gaoler's lodgings to watch her father-in-law [31] on his way to Mass in St Peter-ad-Vincula, dismissed his change of heart as evil and false. 'I pray God,' she said, 'I, nor no friend of mine, die so.' [32]

NOTES

1. *Cal SP Spanish*, vol XI, pp 99–102.
2. *Narratives of the Reformation*, ed Nichols, p 152.
3. Harleian MSS, 353.
4. Ibid, 2342.
5. Pollini, *Historia Ecclesiastica*, pp 260–97.
6. *Queen Jane and Queen Mary*, ed Nichols, pp 9, 11, 15.
7. Ibid, p 12.
8. *Cal SP Spanish*, vol XI, p 151.
9. Ibid.
10. *Queen Jane and Queen Mary*, p 14.
11. *Cal SP Spanish*, vol XI, p 151.
12. Ibid, p 119.
13. Ibid, p 166.
14. Ibid, p 168.
15. Ibid, pp 168–9.
16. Ibid, p 169.
17. Foxe, *Acts and Monuments*, vol VIII, pp 290–1.
18. Ibid, p 419.
19. Godwin, *Annals of England*, p 282.
20. Fuller, *Holy State*, p 307.

21. *Cal SP Spanish*, vol XI, pp 119–25.

22. Ibid, pp 168, 178–9.

23. De Guaras, *The Accession of Queen Mary*, p 104.

24. *Cal SP Spanish*, vol XI, p 184.

25. Tytler, *England under the Reigns of Edward VI and Mary*, vol II, p 225; Holinshed, *Chronicle*, vol IV, p 4.

26. Collins, *Letters and Memorials of State*, pp 22–7.

27. *Cal SP Spanish*, vol XI, pp 185–7.

28. Burnet, *History of the Reformation of the Church of England*, vol III, pt 1, p 325.

29. Lodge, *Portraits of Illustrious Personages in Great Britain*, vol II, pp 2–9.

30. Ibid.

31. *Original Letters*, vol I, p 367; Vertot, *Ambassades de MM de Noailles*, vol II, p 117.

32. *Queen Jane and Queen Mary*, pp 19, 55.

Chapter 2

The Captivity of Lady Jane

NORTHUMBERLAND, Gates and Palmer were followed into St Peter-ad-Vincula by a party of aldermen, who had been summoned by the Council as witnesses so that these important conversions should be vouched for and publicized. The Duke of Somerset's two sons were also there, presumably at Northumberland's request. Before going up to the altar, he turned and addressed the congregation. 'My masters,' he said, 'I let you all to understand that I do most faithfully believe this is the very right and true way, out of which true religion you and I have been seduced these sixteen years past, by the false and erroneous preaching of the new preachers, the which is the only cause of the great plagues and vengeance which hath lit upon the whole realm of England, and now likewise worthily fallen upon me and others, for our unfaithfulness. And I do believe the holy sacrament here present to be most assuredly our Saviour and Redeemer Jesus Christ; and this I pray you all to testify, and pray for me.'[1]

After asking everybody to pardon him, Northumberland spoke to Lord Hertford and his brother, confessed that he had engineered their father's death and begged their forgiveness. He and his companions then received the sacrament. As they returned to the Beauchamp Tower someone remarked that on that very day, forty-one years before, the Duke's father had been beheaded on Tower Hill.[2]

The execution took place at ten o'clock on August 23rd. More than ten thousand people had collected on and round Tower Hill before the condemned men heard Mass at nine. It then became apparent that there was a division in the Dudley family. Of the Duke's five sons, Warwick alone was converted to the old faith, and took the sacrament with Gates, Palmer and his father. Ambrose, Robert, Henry and Guilford remained Protestant; neither then nor later was any attempt made to proselytize them. Northumberland said goodbye to the four youngest before going to the chapel. He controlled himself till Guilford knelt for his blessing; as he kissed his favourite son, he broke down and wept.[3]

When the prisoners came to the altar rails they were addressed by the priest as to their views on the Real Presence. 'Ye must here openly acknowledge and grant your abuse and error therein,' he said, 'and then I assure you you shall receive Him to your salvation, were ye never so detestable an offender.' Northumberland could not speak. Sir John Gates said, 'I confess we have been out of the way a long time, and therefore we are worthily punished; and being sorry, I ask God forgiveness therefore, most humbly – and this is the true religion.' After some further conversation, the priest resumed, 'I would ye should not be ignorant of God's mercy, which is infinite – and let not death offend you, for it is but a little while, ended in one half-hour. What shall I say? I trust to God it shall be but a short passage – though somewhat sharp – out of innumerable mercies into a most pleasant rest – which God grant.'[4]

After the service they went out to walk in the Lieutenant's garden till the time came for them to proceed to the scaffold. There they said goodbye to the friends who had come to see them die, or who were also in captivity. Warwick embraced his father and went back to the Beauchamp Tower. Gates walked up and down with his confessor. Palmer shook hands with one or two gentlemen. And all the time Lord Hertford and his brother stood looking on.[5] At the garden door the Duke met Sir John Gates. 'Sir John,' he said, 'God have mercy upon us, for this day shall end both our lives. And I pray you forgive me whatsoever I have offended; and I forgive you with all my heart.' He could not resist adding, 'Although you and your counsel was a great occasion thereof.' 'Well, my lord,' Gates replied, 'I forgive you as I would be forgiven – and yet you and your authority was the only original cause of all together. But the Lord pardon you, and I pray you forgive me.' Neither could bring himself to shake hands. Bows were exchanged. Then the Duke, elegant in his surcoat of pale grey damask, fell in behind his guards and began the short walk to Tower Hill.[6]

Here the mob would have set upon him, but for the halberdiers. A woman, brandishing a stained handkerchief, rushed between them shouting 'Behold the blood of that worthy man, that good uncle of that excellent King, which now revenges itself upon thee!' and was thrust aside.[7]

When Northumberland had mounted the scaffold, he took off his surcoat and gave it to the executioner, as part of his fee. Leaning upon the rail, he told the 'good people' of London that he was 'a wretched sinner' and 'most justly condemned'. With a return of his old belligerence, he added, 'And yet this act, whereof I die, was not altogether of me, but I was procured and induced thereunto, by others – I was, I say, induced thereunto, by others! Howbeit, God forbid that I should name any man unto you – and therefore, I beseech you, look not for it. I forgive all men.' He then assured his audience that his conversion was genuine and a free act, and reaffirmed his faith, appealing to the priest who had accompanied him to the scaffold to verify this statement. He continued, 'If I had had this belief sooner, I had not come to this pass. Take example of me, and forsake this new doctrine betimes.'

After a description of the miseries caused by Protestantism, Northumberland paused. Then he said, 'I could, good people, rehearse much more. But you know – I have another thing to do, whereunto I must prepare me, for the time draweth away.' He begged the Queen's pardon, and prayed for her and for himself in Latin. As he knelt down, those near heard him murmur, 'I have deserved a thousand deaths.' The white-aproned executioner, who was lame, limped forward and asked him his forgiveness. 'I forgive thee with all my heart,' said the Duke. 'Do thy part without fear.'[8]

His eyes were bandaged. Looking up, he exclaimed, '*In manus tuas, Domine.*' And then, as if this were an insufficient safeguard – as if, in spite of all his precautions, he was seized with a fearful doubt – he burst into a grotesque mingling of the Lord's Prayer and the Hail Mary, crying out, 'O Lord

God my Father! Pray for us poor sinners now and in the hour of our death!'⁹

The bandage slipped and fell. He had to get up for it to be re-tied. In that hideous moment, his courage failed. Then, says an onlooker, 'he surely figured to himself the terrible dreadfulness of death. He smote his hands together, as who would say, "This must be!" – and cast himself on the block.'¹⁰

The lame headsman was competent. A single blow ended John Dudley's life. His companions died bravely, after the usual speeches.¹¹

When the bodies had been removed to St Peter-ad-Vincula – where the Duke was buried above Anne Boleyn and Catherine Howard, and next to Somerset – the crowds swarmed over the place of execution in search of souvenirs. Many had brought their children; and these produced bits of rag, with which they sopped up the blood that was still dripping from between the planks of the scaffold.¹²

ii

The two-storeyed lodgings which Lady Jane spent the last six months of her life are on the left of the main gateway and the Beauchamp Tower, just below Tower Green; they have undergone little or no outward change since she was there, and give the effect of a row of cottages. Lady Throckmorton having left to join her husband, Lady Jane now had only four attendants – Nurse Ellen, Mrs Tilney, Mrs Jacob (her tiring-woman) and the page. They were comfortably housed and well fed – Lady Jane was allowed ninety-three shillings a week and her servants one pound apiece by the Queen's order¹³ – and dined downstairs with Partridge the Gentleman-Gaoler, and his wife, whenever they felt inclined.¹⁴

It seems that for the most part Lady Jane preferred to remain in her own rooms; when the mood took her to join the Partridges, she was given the place of honour, 'at the board's end'. So it was that six days after Northumberland's execution, the anonymous narrator of *Queen Jane and Queen Mary*, who had a post in the Tower, dined with the Partridges and

there met her with Mrs Jacob and her page.* He was slightly
taken aback at finding himself in the presence of royalty;
Lady Jane, who had just heard that although she must be tried
and condemned, she was certain of pardon, was in good spirits.
She desired him and Partridge to put on their caps, and began
the meal by drinking to them both. As they still appeared a
little awestruck, she bade them 'heartily welcome', and then
opened the conversation with the subject uppermost in everyone's mind, leading the talk informally and in her most fluent
and outspoken style.

'The Queen's Majesty,' she said, 'is a merciful princess; I
beseech God she may long continue, and send His bountiful
grace upon her.' 'After that,' says the narrator, 'we fell in discourse of matters of religion; and she asked what he was that
preached at Paul's on Sunday before.' Lady Jane made no
comment when she realized that the preacher was a Catholic.
She went on: 'I pray you – have they Mass in London?' 'Yea,
forsooth,' she was told, 'in some places –' and there was a
pause. 'It may be so,' Lady Jane resumed. 'It is not so strange
as the sudden conversion of the late Duke – for who would
have thought he would have so done?' 'Perchance he thereby
hoped to have had his pardon,' said Partridge's friend.

Lady Jane's whole manner changed. 'Pardon!' she exclaimed passionately, 'woe worth him! He hath brought me
and our stock in most miserable calamity and misery by his
exceeding ambition. But for the answering that he hoped for
life by his turning, though other men be of that opinion, I utterly
am not – for what man is there living, I pray you, although he
had been innocent, that would hope of life in that case, being
in the field against the Queen in person as General, and after
his being so hated and evil spoken of by the commons? And at
his coming into prison so wondered at [abused] as the like
was never heard by any man's time?' No one ventured to
answer, and she swept on, 'Who was judge that he should
hope for pardon, whose life was odious to all men? But what

* There is some evidence, mainly conjectural, that this narrator was
called Rowland Lea; he must have had rank and education, or he
would not have been admitted to dine with Lady Jane.

will ye more? Like as his life was wicked and full of dissimulation, so was his end thereafter.'

Someone seems either to have made an attempt to defend
the Duke, or to describe his last hours, for she continued with
increasing violence, 'Should I, who am young, and in my few
years, forsake my faith for the love of life? Nay, God forbid!
Much more *he* should not, whose fatal course, although he had
lived his just number of years, could not have long continued.'

Once more something was said about Northumberland's being reconciled in the hope of saving his life. Lady Jane replied,
'But life was sweet, it appeared; so he might have lived, you
will say, he did not care how. Indeed, the reason is good,' she
added bitterly, 'for he that would have lived in chains to have
had his life, belike would leave no other mean attempted.'
Then her mood changed. She said, 'But God be merciful to
us! For He sayeth, Whoso denyeth Me before men, I will not
know him in My Father's kingdom.'

'With this and much like talk,' the narrator goes on, 'the
dinner passed away.' At its conclusion he thanked Lady Jane
for her graciousness. 'I thank you,' she replied. 'You are welcome.' And turning to Partridge, she added, 'I thank you sir,
for bringing this gentleman to dinner.' 'Madam,' said the
Gentleman-Gaoler, 'we were somewhat bold, not knowing
that your ladyship dined below until we found your ladyship
there.' Lady Jane then retired, and the two men went about
their duties.[15]

The fact that Lady Jane's conversation was so fully reported, even down to social trivialities, is a proof of the impact
of her personality. A hundred years later, her formidable
volubility and violent frankness were glossed over, only her
'rare and incomparable perfections' remembered,[16] and by the
middle of the seventeenth century she had become 'the wonder
and delight of all who knew her.[17] So it was inevitable that
the Victorians should see her as the 'gentle Jane' of *Lives of
the Tudor and Stuart Princesses* and the dove-like saint of
Little Arthur's England, whose author, writing in the 1840s,
describes her career as follows: 'Some people would have
liked Lady Jane [as Queen] best, first, because their dear

young King Edward had wished her to be Queen; and next, because she was beautiful, virtuous and wise, and, above all, a Protestant . . . She was like him in gentleness, goodness and kindness.'[18]

The meek heroine of Miss Strickland and Lady Callcott would have shrunk from the vigorous young woman who dominated the talk at the Partridges' table, defied and abused her parents, ordered her husband to remain with her against his will and who had no pity on apostates and poltroons.

Of these, Northumberland, as the most eminent and responsible, perished before she could tell him what she thought of him; this was not the case of her first tutor, Dr Harding, who, in the autumn following her reign, was converted to Catholicism, as were many of the more prudent Anglican clergy.

As soon as Lady Jane heard of this defection her disgust and fury burst forth in a letter, generally circulated after Queen Mary's death and printed in Foxe's *Acts and Monuments*. It then became a popular pamphlet, and until the eighteenth century – when the dove-cum-saint view of the author's character began to obtain – was cited as a superb example of pietistic fervour. The Victorians maintained – on no ostensible evidence – that it was not her work, but that of her tutor, Bishop Aylmer, who had left England, remaining abroad till Elizabeth's accession. And as early as 1680 Bishop Burnet speaks of it rather deprecatingly as 'of an extraordinary strain, full of life in the thoughts, and of zeal, *if there is not too much*, in the expressions'.[19]

Her contemporaries, on the other hand, greeted the Harding letter rapturously, as the inspired product of 'an earnest heart', and the work of 'a Christian lady ... not a little aggrieved' by her former preceptor's 'sliding away . . . from the way of truth.'

Opening with a reference to those who put their hand to the plough and then look back, Lady Jane declares, 'I cannot but marvel at thee and lament thy case, who seemed sometime to be the lively member of Christ, but now the deformed imp of the devil; sometime the beautiful temple of God, but now the stinking and filthy kennel of Satan; sometime the unspotted spouse of Christ, but now the unshamefaced paramour of anti-Christ . . . When I consider these things I cannot but . . . cry out upon thee, thou white-livered milksop . . . sink of sin . . . child of perdition . . . . seed of Satan.' After a long rhetorical passage ('Wherefore hast thou instructed others to be strong in Christ, when thou thyself dost now so shamefully shrink, and so horribly abuse the . . . law of the Lord?') Lady Jane enforces her argument with quotations from Baruch, Jeremiah, the Psalms and St Luke, and urges Harding, although 'a miserable wretch', 'to fight manfully, come life, come death; the quarrel is God's and undoubtedly the victory is ours'.

She then reverts to St Paul's descriptions of eternal punishment ('Dost thou not quake and tremble?'), thereafter adopting a more persuasive strain. 'Well, if these terrible and thundering threatenings stir thee to cleave unto Christ . . . let the sweet consolations and promises of the Scriptures encourage thee to take faster hold.' She subjoins a series of quotations from the New Testament and gives examples of 'holy men and women' who 'condemned all torments devised by the tyrants, for their Saviour's sake'.

Now comes the peroration. 'Throw down yourself with the fear of His threatened vengeance, for this so great and heinous an offence . . . Be not ashamed to turn again . . . acknowledging that you have sinned against heaven and earth . . . Be not abashed to . . . weep bitterly with Peter . . . to wash away, out of the sight of God, the filth and mire of your offensive fall . . . Last of all,' she concludes, 'let the last remembrance of the last day be always before your eyes, remembering the terror . . . [of] the runagates and fugitives from Christ . . . and, contrariwise, the inestimable joys prepared for them that . . . have triumphed . . . over all power of darkness.' In a farewell couplet she strikes a cheerful and encouraging note:

Be constant, be constant: fear not for any pain;
Christ hath redeemed thee, and Heaven is thy gain.[20]

This effusion, although not exactly the work of a self-abnegating and sensitive thinker, is clearly that of a 'natural' writer, one who composes partly for her own pleasure and partly because she cannot help it. The sentences soar and explode like rockets: the quotations tumble over one another; the rhetoric is as unselfconscious as it is passionate, exuberant and sincere. Lady Jane's letter may have been 'touched up' by Aylmer or Foxe before publication. Yet the similarity between it and the writer's diatribe against Northumberland needs little emphasis. Such phrases as 'odious to all men', 'woe worth him' and 'wicked and full of dissimulation' have their parallel in 'seed of Satan', 'the filth and mire of your offensive fall' and 'runagates from Christ'. And again, although somewhat dimmed in translation, Lady Jane's Zurich letters show the same fervour, the same headlong enthusiasm for words – while these in their turn are reflected in her outpourings to Ascham about her home life. ('Whether I speak, keep silence, sit, stand or go, eat, drink, be merry or sad, be sewing, playing, dancing, or doing anything else . . .') Although apt to become intoxicated with her own eloquence, Lady Jane could exercise restraint, and that very impressively, when describing events, as in her letter to Queen Mary about Northumberland's plot. She may not have liked writing down that careful and controlled account of her own mistakes; she must have enjoyed giving vent to her condemnation of Harding.

So these first weeks of captivity were perhaps not altogether disagreeable, after the suspense and terror of her nine days' reign. She had leisure to study and compose; and she knew so much classical and religious literature by heart that she could always entertain herself by repeating passages from her favourite authors. Furthermore, however long her captivity might last, she had her cousin's word as a Queen that she would not be put to death. Eventually therefore, she must be set free; she had only to wait until all danger of an anti-Catholic rebellion died down.

Meanwhile Renard, still bent on her destruction, forced the Queen to admit that, technically, 'Jane of Suffolk deserved death according to English law.' Finding Mary resolved on mercy, he suggested that the usurper should be imprisoned in Spain.[21] (No doubt the imprisonment would have been a fatally short one.) This suggestion met with no response, and the Ambassador had to be contented with what he described as the salutary effect of Northumberland's conversion and the spectacle of four more rebel heretics – Cranmer, Sandys, Huntingdon and Cheke – being sent to the Tower. Huntingdon at once set about being converted to Catholicism, with the result that he was freed three weeks after Mary's coronation, which took place on October 1st.[22] Of those already free, the Duchess of Northumberland was fined and allowed to stay in her own house; Suffolk was promised his pardon;[23] North-ampton – who wept continuously during his captivity – was liberated in the second week of September.[24] The wives of Warwick and Robert and Ambrose Dudley were allowed, first to visit and then to stay with their respective husbands in the Beauchamp Tower.[25] Then the five sons and the two brothers of the late Duke were all given 'the liberty of the leads', as of the Lieutenant's garden, now resplendent with autumn roses.[26]

Indoors, Guilford Dudley began to occupy himself with carving a memorial to his family. It was the habit of most prisoners to leave this kind of record, and Guilford's was very elaborate – so much so, that it was never completed. There, on the left-hand wall of the Beauchamp Tower, it is still to be seen. The bear and the ragged staff, facing a lion and sur-rounded by roses and thistles, surmount three and a half lines of verse; on another wall, 'Jane' in large capitals appears. From this inscription the romantic theory of Guilford's devo-tion to his wife has arisen, without regard to the fact that his mother – the mother who had tried to give him everything he asked for, all his life – was also called Jane.*

The composition of verse came hard on Guilford. He began boldly enough:

> *You that these beasts do well behold and see,*
> *May deem with ease wherefore here made they be.*

* *Archaeologia*, vol IV, p 70. This carving has been attributed to Northumberland, who was in the Tower for far too short a time – and in much too agitated a condition – to contemplate such an under-taking. The memorial is a young man's, almost a schoolboy's work; one cannot imagine the Duke wasting his time on, let alone having the inclination for, an occupation of this kind.

The next line opens, 'With borders eke therein' – and then breaks off; the sculptor, perhaps intending to fill in the gap later on, has supplied another : 'The Brother's name who list to search the Crown' – and then abandoned this too ambitious design.

While the Dudleys were submitting to the Queen's mild treatment, plans were made for their public disgrace and condemnation. On November 14th Lady Jane, Cranmer, Guilford, Henry and Ambrose Dudley were summoned to appear at the Guildhall before Judge Morgan, the newly appointed Justice of the Common Pleas.

NOTES

1. *Queen Jane and Queen Mary*, ed Nichols, p 18.
2. Ibid, p 191; *Cal SP Spanish*, vol XI, p 187.
3. Davey, p 307.
4. *Queen Jane and Queen Mary*, p 21.
5. Ibid.
6. Ibid.
7. Godwin, *Annals of England*, p 251.
8. Collins, *Letters and Memorials of State*, pp 22–7.
9. *Antiquarian Repertory*, vol IV, p 503.
10. De Guaras, *The Accession of Queen Mary*, p 108.
11. Holinshed, *Chronicle*, vol IV, p 4.
12. *Antiquarian Repertory*, p 503.
13. Sidney, *Jane the Quene*, p 147.
14. *Queen Jane and Queen Mary*, p 25.
15. Ibid, pp 25–6.
16. Hayward, *Life of Edward VI*, p 421.
17. Burnet, *History of the Reformation of the Church of England*, vol III, pt 1, p 329.
18. Ibid, pp 163–4.
19. Ibid, vol II, pt 1, p 424.
20. Ibid, vol VI, pp 418–22.
21. *Cal SP Spanish*, vol XI, p 194.
22. *Queen Jane and Queen Mary*, p 27.
23. *Cal SP Spanish*, vol XI, p 196.
24. Ibid.
25. *Acts of the Privy Council*, vol IV, p 317.
26. *Queen Jane and Queen Mary*, p 27.

Chapter 3

The Trial and Condemnation of Lady Jane

T H E number of trials for high treason that took place during the first weeks of Mary's reign seems to have drawn her attention to the prejudice with which they were conducted. When she appointed Morgan to try the Dudleys, Cranmer and Lady Jane, she directed him to 'administer the law impartially . . . notwithstanding the old error amongst you, which did not admit any witness to speak, or anything else to be in favour of the adversary [prisoner] . . . It is my pleasure that whatever can be produced in favour of the subject shall be heard.'[1]

This attempt to rectify legal procedure had no effect; the old customs continued to prevail; it was left to the Queen to revoke sentence of death to a fine or imprisonment, or both.

For many weeks the Duchess of Northumberland had been trying to secure a pardon for her five sons,[2] with the result that Lord Robert was not summoned to the Guildhall; he and Warwick, who had already been sentenced, were to remain in the Tower, on the assumption that eventually they would be released, while an example was made of their brothers, as far as condemnation was concerned.

The official sentence for men committing high treason was that of hanging, drawing and quartering, and for women, to be burnt; in the case of persons of high rank this was afterwards commuted to beheading for both sexes; the offenders could count on the comparatively merciful death, provided they pleaded for it in the proper manner; but as the law stood, the more horrible sentences had to be passed.

When Lady Jane, the Dudley brothers and Cranmer left the Tower to take barge for the Guildhall, they themselves were virtually sure of mercy. Those who, unaware of Mary's intentions, watched their progress, saw Jane and Guilford as innocent victims of the Queen's vengeance; for they had no active share in the rebellion, while Henry and Ambrose had appeared against her in the field and Cranmer had concurred (although reluctantly) in the plot to deprive her of the throne.[3] So it was that the Londoners began to feel pity and indignation for the young couple, and became interested in them both. As they left the barge to walk to the Guildhall, every detail of the procession was carefully noted.[4]

Some four hundred halberdiers lined the street; guards separated the prisoners from one another. Lady Jane, as became her rank, appeared first, her two gentlewomen walking behind her. She was dressed in a black gown, turned back underneath an overskirt of black velvet; on her head was a black satin hood with jet trimming; her little Prayer Book hung at her girdle; she carried another, reading from it as she walked along.[5]

The course of the trial was formal and extremely brief. The prisoners pleaded guilty. Judge Morgan then pronounced the sentences with all their ghastly details.[6]

Lady Jane showed no emotion; at some point in the procedure she looked at Morgan. He never forgot that look.[7] He could not escape the remembrance of the pale, freckled face under the black hood and the large, widely spaced brown eyes fixed steadily upon him.[8]

The edge of the axe turned towards the little group at the bar, the Court rose and the prisoners were conducted to Temple Stairs. When Lady Jane rejoined her attendants in the Gentleman-Gaoler's lodgings, there was an outburst of weeping. She tried to console them; then she said, 'Remember – I am innocent, and did not deserve this sentence. But I should not have accepted the crown.'[9] She had just passed her sixteenth birthday.

No comment was made, in writing at least, by those who saw the executioner follow the prisoners to the water's edge. 'Arraigned and condemned', 'judgement to die' – so run the laconic entries.[10] Renard was a little worried. The criminals were apparently doomed – but, 'when execution is to take place is uncertain, for though the Queen is truly irritated against the Duke of Suffolk, it is believed that Jane will not die.' A few days later he reported that Suffolk had expressed a wish to be converted, and that 'the Queen has therefore remitted his composition to £20,000, and reinstated him by means of a general pardon. As for Jane, I am told that her life is safe, though several people are trying to encompass her death.'[11] It was all rather disappointing; he turned towards the more promising business of the Queen's marriage.

Three days after Lady Jane's trial the Council, alarmed by Mary's avowed inclination towards marriage with Prince Philip, begged her, in the strongest terms, to wed an Englishman; although his name was not mentioned, it was obvious that this could be no other than Courtenay. Mary replied that if she were forced to take a husband she disliked – and she had already made it clear that she had no use at all for the last sprig of the White Rose – 'it would be her death'. On November 20th she solemnly promised Renard that she would never marry Courtenay, who was now making up for his years in the Tower by hurrying round the brothels of the city.[12] On the 21st Titian's portrait of Philip was dispatched from Madrid, with instructions from the Emperor that it must be looked at, as in the case of all that artist's work, from a distance.[13] On the 25th he wrote formally to the Council, outlining the terms of the alliance.[14]

If Mary had married Courtenay – and there is little doubt that she would have been as unhappy with this vain and foolish young man as with the husband who made no attempt to conceal his distaste for her – Lady Jane might have lived to maturity. Her death was one of the indirect results of Mary's falling in love with Philip before she even saw his picture. When the Queen peremptorily told the Lords that her marriage was her own affair, she had already announced her decision to Renard, and, kneeling to the Host in a passion of tears, taken the fair-haired Habsburg for her husband in her heart.[15] If this ageing, obstinate, pathetic spinster had ever read the legend of Joffroi Rudel and the Lady of Tripoli, it would not have given her pause; for she was simply reversing the pattern of Henry VIII's rejection of her mother when she told Renard that she had God's approval of the marriage.

As Courtenay abandoned his hopes of grandeur and his half-hearted courtship of the Princess Elizabeth, those of the Council who had not been bribed or won over by Renard gave their mistress a last warning. Mary replied that she would rather die than marry anyone but Philip, the terms of the contract were arranged and the date of his arrival settled.[16] By the beginning of December, a number of people were in a state of undeclared rebellion, not only against the Spanish marriage but against the Queen's religious restorations. Priests were stoned: a dead dog with a shaven crown was hurled through the window of Mary's bedchamber;[17] and a French statesman, instructed by Henri II to break up the alliance, told the English Ambassador in Paris that wherever the Spaniards came they brought 'bondage and misery – even so must you look to be in England'.[18]

As the popular tide rose against the Queen in wave after wave of crudely expressed insularity and Protestantism, Lady Jane's pardon was delayed. On this point Mary's intentions remained unchanged; but she could not set her cousin free until she herself was married, the old faith reinstated and an Anglo-Spanish dynasty established. Meanwhile, she befriended Katherine and Mary Grey, giving them allowances and posts at Court.[19]

So Lady Jane continued under sentence of death at the stake. She had books, writing materials and leave to walk in the garden – even, under escort, as far as Tower Hill – as had Guilford and his brothers. There is no record of their meeting; naturally this was not allowed. But the Lieutenant of the Tower, Sir John Bridges, was an easy-going man and apt to turn a blind eye when kindness prompted. Jane became very fond of him and thought of herself as his 'true friend'.[20] It is possible therefore, that he allowed her and Guilford to correspond, or at least to send one another messages.

ii

A few weeks after her trial Lady Jane's liberties were curtailed, and she was no longer allowed to leave the Gentleman-Gaoler's lodgings; presently she fell ill. This confinement was probably caused by the alarms arising from the unrest within the kingdom, which resulted in the diminution of Queen Mary's popularity. The Council believed that although no one had wanted Jane to be Queen, she or the Princess Elizabeth might be made the figurehead of a rebellion against the Spanish marriage by the ultra-Protestant party. As Mary's hold on the people sank away that of Elizabeth rose, and with it the first public manifestations of her powers of enchantment, so that she was seen as the dangerous and fascinating enemy of the régime, while Lady Jane was almost forgotten, with the result that on December 17th Sir John Bridges was told to let her renew her walks in the Tower garden, 'at his discretion'.[21] On the same day Renard reported to the Emperor that 'the Greys and the Suffolks are planning a revolution'.[22]

By the Greys he meant Suffolk's brothers, Lord John and Lord Thomas, who had taken little or no share in Northumberland's conspiracy, but were now about to join the head of their house in a venture which had much more general support than Northumberland's – that of forcing the Queen to abandon Prince Philip by threatening to depose her in favour of either Elizabeth or Jane.

On this point all except those in the pay of the Emperor were agreed; on that of religion, the country was split, and its divisions were innumerable. In London, where Protestantism prevailed, the Catholic minority took every opportunity to humiliate disgraced and imprisoned heretics, although no demonstrations were made against Lady Jane and the Dudleys; in the north, then the largest Catholic area, a few Protestants defied the Queen's edicts and continued to abuse the Papists. In every town and village – sometimes in a single street – similar disagreements were abusively and violently expressed. The reception of Dr Sandys on his way to the Tower is a good example of this widespread divergence. As he rode through

Tower Hill Street a woman screamed, 'Fie on thee, thou knave, thou traitor, thou heretic!' From the opposite house another exclaimed, 'Fie on thee, neighbour! Thou art not worthy to be called a woman, railing upon this gentleman whom thou knowest not.' Turning to Sandys, she continued, 'God be thy comfort, and give thee strength to stand in God's cause, even to the end.' Her prayer was granted. Sandys' release followed in a few months, and he went abroad, remaining there till Mary's death.[23]

The instinct to speak out was stimulated by the news of Prince Philip's arrival, which presently united Catholic and Protestant landowner and labourer, in furious condemnation. On Christmas Eve a Cornish peasant, John Combe, told his drinking companions, Cowlyn and Jackman, 'I have heard and seen this day that thing I have not seen in four years before, for I have, thanked be God, heard Mass and received holy bread and holy water.' 'I would all priests were hanged!' cried Cowlyn. 'God forbid,' said Combe piously, 'for the Queen's Grace hath granted it.' 'The Queen, a vengeance take her!' Cowlyn exclaimed, and Jackman concurred with 'Amen!' Cowlyn pursued, 'I may say it well, for before New Year's Day outlandish men will come upon our lands, for there be some at Plymouth already.' 'Before twelve months,' Jackman added, 'you shall see all houses of religion up again, with the Pope's laws.' 'We ought not,' was Cowlyn's conclusion, 'to have a woman bear the sword.' 'If a woman bear the sword, my Lady Elizabeth ought to have it first,' said Jackman.[24]

Indeed the Spaniards, it was well known, were wicked, cruel and, in more than one sense, rapacious. 'How wouldst thou say,' inquired a Kentish gentleman of 'one Pipit, his workman', 'if a Spanish soldier should ravish thy wife before thy face?' 'I would rather cut off the Prince of Spain's head myself,' was the satisfactory answer.[25]

In the same week, Mr Iseley of Ightham told the smith who was shoeing his horse that 'the Spaniards are coming into the realm with harness [armour] and hand-guns, and will make us Englishmen worse than enemies, and viler – for this realm shall be brought into such bondage as never afore.' The cautious smith said nothing till his work was done and the young squire, swinging into his saddle, ordered him to call upon his neigh- bours to rise. 'Why,' he replied slowly, 'these be marvellous words, for we shall all be hanged if we stir.' 'Ye shall have help enough,' Iseley assured him, 'for people are already up in Devonshire and Cornwall, Hampshire and other counties' – and rode away.[26]

In all this indignant discussion Lady Jane's name never arose; and so in the weeks succeeding her trial she had reason to believe that she would be pardoned soon. According to the French Ambassador, the Queen was still determined on her release.[27] Yet as the weeks went by and nothing happened, she began to give up hope and tried to resign herself. To this period of her imprisonment her inscriptions on the wall of her room can be attributed. They have long since disappeared; when what may be described as her canonization began they could still be seen, and were reproduced in the memoirs and chronicles of the time. Both were in Latin; they have come down to posterity in rhyming couplets.

> *To mortals' common fate thy mind resign,*
> *My lot today tomorrow may be thine.*

And:

> *Whilst God assists us, envy bites in vain,*
> *If God forsake us, fruitless all our pain –*
> *I hope for light after the darkness.*[28]

And now darkness began to fall over England. After Renard had been told that many Protestants were prepared to risk their lives rather than that the Spanish marriage should take place,[29] the machinery of propaganda was set in motion. In a sermon at Westminster, Bishop Gardiner dwelt on the resultant 'wealth and enriching of the realm' and the splendour of the Queen's dowry ('thirty-thousand ducats, with all the Low Countries of Flanders'), tactlessly adding, 'We are much bounden to thank God that so noble, worthy and famous a Prince would vouch- safe so to humble himself, as in this marriage.'[30]

The haughty nobles were enraged; the City fathers became

very anxious; and in the country districts such persons as Jackman, Pipit and the smith of Ightham abandoned religious dispute, polished up their weapons and began to look for leaders. While the London schoolboys were snowballing the first batch of 'outlandish' envoys,[31] Peter Carew in the West and Sir Thomas Wyatt in Kent were organizing rebellion on a large scale.

Renard dismissed these demonstrations as negligible, the work of a few heretics and – inevitably – of the French Ambassador;[32] the Council took them more seriously. On the day that Renard presented them with a further bribe of thirty thousand crowns they summoned Carew from Devonshire and arrested some half-dozen Protestant nobles.[33] Meanwhile the Queen showed her distrust by making the Lords sign a paper in which each declared his approval of the match.[34] On January 18th, 1554, Renard reported that Suffolk had not yet put his name to this document, and that Carew, ignoring the Queen's command, had announced his intention of throwing the next contingent of Spaniards into the sea.[35] By the 23rd Mary had raised a force of 8,000 men and written Philip a reassuring and affectionate letter, to which she added the ominous postscript: 'Bring your own cooks.' On the same day that a young man describing himself as Edward VI appeared in London and was sent to the Tower, the egregious Courtenay put his services at Wyatt's disposal.[36]

It was characteristic of the situation into which the Queen and Renard had plunged the kingdom that Sir Thomas Wyatt, the only son of the poet, soldier and diplomat, should be a Catholic who had risen to fight for her in the preceding summer. With his famous father, this wild young man – he had been sent to the Fleet for brawling under Henry VIII – had travelled much in Spain, where he 'imbibed an utter detestation' of its inhabitants and their ways.[37] He now visited the Duke of Suffolk at Sheen and obtained the promise of his and his brothers' support, apparently on the understanding that Lady Jane should be put forward as the claimant to the throne in his forthcoming proclamation.[38] At least, this was what Suffolk understood by the transaction. Wyatt, while not wishing to desert either his faith or his Queen, intended to force Mary to abandon the marriage by using Jane (and, failing her, Elizabeth) as a threat. Neither seems to have considered what Jane's fate would be if the rebellion failed. In fact, Wyatt was sure of victory. Everyone appeared to be on his side.

The planning of the revolt was faultless. Wyatt left Sheen for Kent on January 23rd, having arranged with Suffolk that the Duke should issue his anti-Spanish proclamation in Leicester and Coventry on the 26th. On the same day that Wyatt's heralds read out a similar appeal in Maidstone, Carew's would be heard in Plymouth and Exeter. Then their three forces would close in on London.[39] Suffolk now got into touch with Huntingdon, who promised that he would join in the rebellion by raising his tenants in Ashby de la Zouch.[40] Huntingdon at once reported these plans to the Council, who between six and seven on the morning of the 25th sent a messenger to Sheen, requiring the Duke to return to London immediately. 'Marry,' Suffolk replied, 'I was coming to Her Grace. Ye may see I am booted and spurred, ready to ride – I will but break my fast and go.' The messenger was then taken to another room, where he was given a drink and bribed to stay quiet while the Duke left the house, picking up his brothers at Enfield.[41] He proceeded via Stony Stratford to Leicester, reaching the city on the 29th. Here the Mayor, having heard his proclamation (in which Lady Jane was not mentioned) said, 'My lord, I trust Your Grace meaneth no hurt to the Queen's Majesty?' 'No!' replied Suffolk, laying his hand on his sword. 'He that would her any hurt, I would this sword were through his heart. For she is the mercifullest prince, as I have truly found, that ever reigned, in whose defence I am, and will be, ready to die at her foot.'[42]

Almost at the same moment Wyatt was saying to his followers in Maidstone, 'We mind nothing less than anywise to touch Her Grace, but to serve her ... according to our duties.' When someone suggested that he might 'restore the right religion'. Wyatt replied, 'Whist! You may not so much as name religion, for that will withdraw from us the hearts of many. You must only make your quarrel for overrunning by strangers.'[43]

As Wyatt left Maidstone a counter-proclamation was issued at West Malling, in which Lady Jane was named as the Queen's rival, and it was added that Wyatt intended to restore her, with the result that the citizens declared for Mary.[44] On the 26th the Government proclamation appeared in London, reaching Kent on the 27th and the other rebellious counties on the 28th. In it Suffolk, Carew and Wyatt were described as conspirators and traitors to the crown, who had 'raised certain evil disposed persons ... to Her Grace's destruction, and to advance the Lady Jane ... and Guilford Dudley.'[45]

On the 27th Mary sent the Duke of Norfolk into Kent with a strong force, most of whom deserted to Wyatt; Norfolk fled and Wyatt proceeded to Rochester. In London the Council began to consider abandoning the Queen and declaring for the Princess Elizabeth. Meanwhile Huntingdon, steeped, as ever, in treachery and dishonour, flung himself at Mary's feet and implored her to allow him enough men and ammunition to pursue and capture Suffolk, who was hourly expecting him as an ally. Mary give her permission and Huntingdon, having sent a message to Suffolk to say that he was on his way, reached Leicester on the 30th to find that the Duke had left for Coventry with 1,400 men, after bringing over the larger city to his side. Before setting off Suffolk had desired Bowyer, one of his gentlemen, to write to the Mayor and Corporation of Northampton, enclosing his proclamation. Bowyer was arming the Duke, who, he says, 'being chafed at something suddenly, gave me a little blow with the back of his hand – whether he thought it had been his armourer or no, I cannot tell'. Bowyer deserted his master in a huff and presently informed on him to the Privy Council.[46]

Huntingdon managed to get to Coventry before Suffolk, with the result that the Duke arrived there to find the citizens armed to resist him and the gates barred. His men began to desert. He then retreated to his manor of Astley, five miles away.[47]

By this time Wyatt had reached Gravesend, where Sir Edward Hastings, failing to stop his progress, asked for a parley, at which Wyatt required the custody of the Tower and of the

Queen's person. When Hastings, having rejected this demand, returned to London, Mary prepared for civil war, while Wyatt proceeded to Deptford, and then retreated to Kingston-on-Thames. Next day, February 5th, he advanced to St James' Park, where the greater part of his forces was routed by Pembroke and Sir Humphrey Clinton. With a small following he broke away and passed through Charing Cross, Fleet Street and Ludgate, attempting to recruit the citizens, who had locked themselves into their houses.[48]

The attack on her marriage plans had roused the Queen to angry yet calculating defiance. Having assured a deputation from the Commons that it should never interfere with their liberties – 'for I am already married to this commonweal and the faithful members of the same, the espousal ring whereof I have on my finger'[49] – she said to Renard, 'I consider myself His Highness' wife. I will never take another husband, I would rather lose my crown and my life.'[50] She then rode to the Guildhall to wait for news of the battle. There, hearing shouts of 'All is lost – away, away!' she told her terrified attendants, "Fall to prayer – I warrant you we shall hear better news anon.' And in a magnificent speech from the balcony she appealed to the citizens to support her. While she was being rapturously acclaimed Wyatt was captured at Temple Bar. At five o'clock on the evening of February 6th Sir Henry Jerningham brought him to the Tower.[51]

All this time Huntingdon, unaware of Wyatt's defeat, was searching for Suffolk, who had been hidden by one of his keepers in a hollow tree at Astley, while Lord John Grey concealed himself under a bundle of hay near the church. (Lord Thomas had escaped, and was on his way to the Welsh border.) For two days and nights the wretched Duke crouched, shivering, in the darkness. Lord John's hiding-place was sniffed out by a dog, and he was placed under escort. Still the pitiless Huntingdon pursued his prey, preparing, as it seemed, to range the park indefinitely. Then the keeper, fearing for his own life, led him to the tree. Suffolk crawled out and collapsed at his enemy's feet.[52]

Huntingdon delivered him up to the Lieutenant of the

Tower a few hours before Wyatt entered it by Traitor's Gate. He went on to Westminster, to be received, with the rest of the Council, by the Queen. In her deep man's voice she thanked them, and gave Pembroke – who had sworn that he would not look upon her face again until the rebels were crushed – a diamond ring. He at once burst into tears, as did several of his fellows. Renard, having cynically observed this scene, sat down to write to the Emperor, that, at last, 'Jane of Suffolk and her husband are to lose their heads'.[53]

NOTES

1. Jardine, *State Trials*, vol I, p 93.
2. *Cal SP Spanish*, vol XI, p 279.
3. Chapman, *The Last Tudor King*.
4. Holinshed, *Chronicle*, vol IV, p 23.
5. Ibid.
6. Ibid.
7. Florio, p 63.
8. Wriothesley, vol II, p 104; *Queen Jane and Queen Mary*, p 29.
9. *Cal SP Spanish*, vol XI, pp 289, 356.
10. Ibid, p 363.
11. De Noailles, vol II, p 395.
12. *Cal SP Spanish*, vol XI, p 395.
13. Ibid, pp 372, 384, 386.
14. Ibid, p 326.
15. Ibid, p 395.
16. Ibid, p 444.
17. Tytler, *England under the Reigns of Edward VI and Mary*, vol II, p 269.
18. Chapman, *Two Tudor Portraits*.
19. *Queen Jane and Queen Mary*, p 30; Harleian MSS, 2342.
20. *Acts of the Privy Council*, vol IV, p 279.
21. *Cal SP Spanish*, vol XI, p 441.
22. Holinshed, vol IV, p 112.
23. *Antiquarian Repertory*, vol III, p 112.
24. *Cal SP Domestic* (1547–1580), p 57.
25. Tytler, vol II, p 278.
26. Vertot, *Ambassades de MM de Noailles*, vol II, p 97.

27. *Archaeologia*, vol III, p 70.

28. *Cal SP Spanish*, vol III, p 395.

29. *Queen Jane and Queen Mary*, p 35.

30. Ibid.

31. *Cal SP Spanish*, vol IV, pp 16, 29–30.

32. Ibid.

33. Ibid.

34. Ibid.

35. Ibid.

36. Ibid, pp 38–9.

37. *Archaeologia*, vol III, pp 65–105.

38. Ibid.

39. *Queen Jane and Queen Mary*, pp 123, 182–5; *Antiquarian Repertory*, vol III, pp 65–105.

40. *Queen Jane and Queen Mary*, pp 123, 182–5.

41. Ibid, p 37.

42. Ibid, p 123.

43. *Antiquarian Repertory*, vol III, pp 65–105.

44. *Cal SP Spanish*, vol XII, p 55.

45. *Queen Jane and Queen Mary*, p 182.

46. Ibid.

47. Ibid.

48. Ibid, pp 4–5; *Antiquarian Repertory*, vol III, pp 65–105; Holinshed, vol. IV, pp. 14–17.

49. *Antiquarian Repertory*, vol III, pp 65–105.

50. *Cal SP Spanish*, vol XIII, p 79.

51. *Queen Jane and Queen Mary*, p 182; *Antiquarian Repertory*, vol III, pp 65–105; Holinshed, vol IV, pp 14–17.

52. *Queen Jane and Queen Mary*, p 122; Grafton, *Chronicle*, vol IV, p 539.

53. *Cal SP Spanish*, vol XII, p 86.

Chapter 4

The Execution of Lady Jane

Two days after Wyatt, Suffolk and his brothers (Lord Thomas had been captured near the Welsh border) were brought into the Tower, Lady Jane and Lord Guilford Dudley were told to prepare for death on the following morning.[1]

Although Lady Jane was strictly guarded and had far less chance of escape than if she had been imprisoned in the Bell or the Beauchamp Tower, she was not cut off from the outside world. The Partridges and their friends would have kept her informed of events. She was therefore able to follow the course of the rebellion; and during those three weeks she saw her own death come nearer every day.

This girl of sixteen, vital, brilliant and passionately absorbed in the pursuit of learning and the discoveries of the intellect, loved life; she did not want to die. And now that death appeared inevitable and all hope of pardon gone, she was afraid. The terror of violence and butchery, implemented by hideous tales of men and women with whose writhing bodies the headsman had bungled, seems to have overwhelmed her. The record of that last agony is contained in the prayer she wrote for herself, published some twenty years later.[2]

And in the midst of the struggle came temptation – an offer of escape. If she would become a Catholic, she need not die. That this offer was made or at least hinted at, is proved by Renard's account of Queen Mary's actions and by those of the persons who were with Lady Jane during the days immediately preceding her execution.

Her prayer begins with a description of herself as a 'poor and desolate woman ... overwhelmed with miseries, vexed with temptations, and grievously tormented with the long imprisonment of this vile mass of clay, my sinful body'. Then comes a passage in which resignation is attempted, ending with the writer's cry that she might not 'deny Thee, my God, being too low brought ... and blaspheme Thee, my Lord and Saviour'.

'Be unto me', she goes on, 'a strong tower of defence ... Suffer me not to be tempted above my power.' She prays for liberty – it may be that while she was doing so the fate of the Wyatt rising was still uncertain – and then sinks into doubt and despair. 'How long wilt Thou be absent? For ever? Is Thy mercy clean gone ... and Thy promise come utterly to an end? Why dost Thou make so long tarrying?'

Lady Jane's rooms looked out on the place of the scaffold. It is not over-fanciful to imagine her staring at it in the intervals of writing, 'I am Thy workmanship, created in Christ Jesus ... Assuredly, as Thou canst, so Thou wilt, deliver me when it shall please Thee ... for Thou knowest better what is good for me than I do; therefore do with me in all things what Thou wilt ... Only, in the meantime, arm me, I beseech Thee ... that I may stand fast.' The penultimate passage is hopeful. 'I am assuredly persuaded that it cannot be but well, all that Thou doest.'

That hope was justified; she was delivered from temptation, and thus from fear, so that before the news came that she was to be beheaded, she was not only ready but glad to end what she now thought of as her 'woeful days'.[3] Perhaps this was because the greatest and perhaps the only real pleasure in her life – that of intellectual and spiritual revelation – had been taken from her. The happy hours spent listening to the rather solemn discussions of Queen Katharine Parr's circle or to kind Dr Aylmer's discourses on faith and works were long past; as were those when she had first conjured up the spirit of a man condemned eighteen centuries ago, and heard him talking to his pupils with the cup of hemlock in his hand. Indeed, their circumstances were curiously similar. He too had been shown a means of escape and refused it. 'I have been condemned,' he said, 'by due process of law, and it would be wrong to do anything to avoid punishment ... Think of justice first, that you may be justified before the princes of the world below ... Now you depart in innocence.'[4]

Lady Jane, who never forgot that in accepting the crown, she had, in her own phrase, neglected God, submitted to the Queen's justice for the same reasons as Socrates submitted to that of the Athenian oligarchs. She might have replied to her weeping ladies as he did to Cebes when the younger man compared death to a hobgoblin sent to frighten children in the dark. 'The soul departs to the invisible world; there arriving, she is sure of bliss and is released from the error and folly of men, their fears and wild passions ... and for ever dwells ... in company with the gods.'

The Renaissance scholar who had been trained to adopt the attitude and behaviour of the Greek philosophers, visualized that future existence as clearly as they did, but in a more concrete setting. To such as Lady Jane, the sea of glass mingled with fire, the jewelled walls of the golden city, the gates of fine pearl, the enraptured angels, the white robes of those who had come out of great tribulation, were as real as the Crown Imperial of the realm, or the block and the axe, or the coffin waiting for her in St Peter-ad-Vincula. In a very little while she would enter into that kingdom where, according to one of her contemporaries, 'your gladness, your mirth, shall be perpetual', and where she would receive a glorious and incorruptible crown.[5]

Yet as she was writing her farewell letters and making her final preparations, her death was still in question. In the last days of the rebellion it dawned on Renard and the Emperor that even now Queen Mary might prevent it; they began to organize their campaign accordingly. 'Let the Queen's clemency be accompanied by a little severity', suggested Charles, and on February 7th Renard despondently replied that although the execution of Jane and her husband had been fixed for the 9th, he was not certain that it would take place, in spite of the fact that Her Majesty's foolish clemency had been so abused.[6] Suffolk, imploring mercy and laying all the blame on Carew (who had escaped overseas) and Wyatt, did not mention his daughter as having been proclaimed. He, his brothers and

Wyatt were to die; Courtenay was in the Tower and Elizabeth would soon be on her way there; in Kent fifty officers and twenty-two soldiers had been hanged.[7] Yet this holocaust would be of no avail if Jane of Suffolk and her husband were allowed to survive.

At last Renard obtained a private audience with the Queen, whose attitude was deplorably mild. She spoke of God's mercy rather than of punishment: of the defeat of heresy rather than of revenge. Renard said something about 'strict justice' and she agreed. 'There has been much negligence,' he went on in his severest manner, and urged the necessity of executing Courtenay and Elizabeth. 'After which,' he concluded, 'Your Majesty need have no fear for your crown, as Jane of Suffolk and Guilford are to be beheaded and the whole house of Suffolk obliterated by the execution of the three brothers, whose death, as heretics, will contribute to the firm re-establishment of religion.'[8]

Renard's assumption that Jane's and Guilford's fate was settled may have irritated the Queen; for a long argument ensued, in which he eventually persuaded her to maintain her decision to execute them.[9] He need not have concerned himself. Three members of the Council - Arundel, Winchester and Pembroke - were even more determined than Renard that the living proofs of their treason should be removed; only so could they be sure of holding power under the new régime. Thus, according to a contemporary, 'They that ... caused the Lady Mary to be proclaimed a bastard ... afterwards became counsellors ... of the innocent Lady Jane's death.'[10]

It was in any case necessary that this boy and girl should die; while they lived, there could be no peace in England, if only because Lady Jane, having been proclaimed Queen, was more likely than Princess Elizabeth to become the excuse for another Protestant rebellion. Furthermore, her and Guilford's existence was bound to delay, if it might not actually prevent, the Spanish marriage. The Emperor was not likely to allow Prince Philip to leave until heresy, as represented by Jane, Guilford, Suffolk and Wyatt, was cut out of the body politic.

(Charles did not, at this time, doubt that their executions would be followed by those of Elizabeth and Courtenay.)

So the Queen had no choice. She made one last effort to befriend Lady Jane by trying to save her soul. She sent her own confessor to the Tower in the hope that he would be able to convert her cousin. In this Mary was not so deluded as it might seem. Dr Feckenham was a very remarkable man; indeed he might be described as a phenomenon.

ii

It is ironical that one of the most eminent English Catholic priests of the sixteenth century should have become famous in history, first because he tried and failed to convert Lady Jane, and then because, within an hour of her death, she accepted him as a friend. In 1554 Feckenham was thirty-nine and at the height of his powers. Born of yeoman stock, he became a monk and in 1539 accepted the Royal Supremacy, thus obtaining a benefice and the chaplaincy to the Bishop of Worcester. In 1547 he was sent to the Tower for preaching an anti-Protestant sermon, where he remained till Queen Mary's accession. In October of that year he was chosen to defend the doctrine of the Real Presence and of transubstantiation in a public debate, thereafter becoming Dean of St Paul's and Abbot of Westminster, where, according to a contemporary, 'he did not insist much upon monastic regularities'.[11] A kind, clever and amazingly tolerant man – he pleaded with Queen Mary for Princess Elizabeth's life, and when Westminster reverted to the reformed faith stayed on in order to arrange the transference of property – he made many converts and was popular with both Catholics and Protestants. (In view of this success, an embittered Calvinist's description of him as 'crafty' may be discounted.[12]) Feckenham was therefore the obvious choice as a proselytizer for Lady Jane, and his effect on her, although not what he had hoped for, rather surprising.

Feckenham's first interview with Lady Jane took place on the 8th of February. In spite of her horror of Papists she received him courteously. He said, 'Madam, I lament your heavy case. Yet I doubt not that you bear out this sorrow with a constant and patient mind.' She replied, 'You are welcome to me, sir, if your coming be to give me Christian exhortation.' [13]

This was promising enough. A long conversation ensued, from which Feckenham concluded that, given time, he would be able to effect another and really sensational conversion. He therefore went to the Queen and asked for three days' postponement of execution, upon which she replied that if Lady Jane became a Catholic she should be reprieved. Feckenham, now on his mettle, hurried back to the Tower with the good news. Jane listened in silence. Then she said smiling, 'Alas! sir – it was not my desire to prolong my days. As for death, I utterly despise it, and, Her Majesty's pleasure being such, I willingly undergo it.' To Feckenham's insistence on the reprieve, she replied, 'You are much deceived if you think I have any desire of longer life, for I assure you, since the time you went from me the time hath been so odious to me that I long for nothing so much as death. Neither did I wish the Queen to be solicited for such a purpose.' [14]

Feckenham, confident in his own powers of debate, then suggested a public conference. Jane said, 'This disputation may be fit for the living, but not for the dying. Leave me to make my peace with God.' [15] Feckenham persuaded her to change her mind, and the debate took place in the chapel in the presence of the Tower officials and, presumably, a shorthand-writer, who recorded its principal points. The disputants began with the accepted formalities. Feckenham said, 'I am here come to you at this present, sent from the Queen and her Council, to instruct you in the true doctrine of the right faith; although I have so great confidence in you, that I shall have, I trust, little to travail with you much therein.'

Jane replied, 'Forsooth, I heartily thank the Queen's Highness, which is not unmindful of her humble subject; and I hope, likewise, that you no less will do your duty therein both truly and faithfully, according to that you were sent for.' [16]

The ensuing discussion followed a set pattern and lasted several hours. Its gist, as recorded by Foxe, naturally shows the Protestant heroine in the ascendant. Feckenham's powers were equally impressive, and, in view of his age and experience, better documented. The martyrologist tries to show him at a disadvantage, by reporting his shift from one point of doctrine to another. (One may be sure that he reverted to the former aspect later on.) After a series of deadlocks on faith and works, this oddly assorted pair of combatants turned to the sacraments. 'How many are there?' Feckenham inquired. 'Two,' Lady Jane replied, 'the one the sacrament of baptism, and the other the sacrament of the Lord's supper.' 'No, there are seven,' retorted Feckenham. 'By what scripture find you that?' said Jane sharply. 'Well, we will talk of that hereafter,' was the evasive answer, 'but what is signified by your two sacraments?' And thence the debate reached its climax with the dogma of transubstantiation, which was discussed fruit-lessly and at length.[17]

At last Feckenham had to acknowledge that he was beaten. 'I am sorry for you,' he said, as they parted, 'for I am sure that we two shall never meet [ie, in the next world].'

'True it is,' Lady Jane replied in her most forceful and fluent style, 'that we shall never meet, except God turn your heart; for I am assured, unless you repent and turn to God, you are in evil case.' She added more gently, 'And I pray God, in the bowels of His mercy, to send you His Holy Spirit – for He hath given you His great gift of utterance, if it pleased Him also to open the eyes of your heart.'[18]

Still Feckenham was not ready to give in – might he accompany her to the scaffold? She consented, he went away, and the preparations for her execution were resumed.

For many years after her death Lady Jane's Calvinist admirers gloated over the failure of what they described as Feckenham's 'contrivances and artifices'.[19] Yet in another sense he did triumph; for from her last speeches and actions it becomes clear that her abhorrence of Papists had been considerably weakened, if not destroyed. She saw in Feckenham all the qualities she most admired; and she was thus bewildered and alarmed, not by his doctrinal arguments (those were wicked and absurd) but by the fact that such a person must be barred from the Paradise she was about to enter. The majority of

Protestants with whom she had had to do had shown themselves corrupt, ruthless, cowardly and brutal. This man, while standing for the forces of evil, was gentle, wise and virtuous – and now, through a piety which she recognized unwillingly, to be as genuine as her own, had become her only friend. Why, otherwise should the time have seemed so odiously long when he left her to plead with the Queen? And why did she wish him to be with her at the last? She was, as she presently confessed, much disturbed. If Feckenham was not a bad man, then there must be other Catholics who were good, however mistaken, however unfortunately doomed. Her conceptions of right and wrong were suddenly assailed; if she had been allowed two more weeks instead of two days to live, she might have become very unhappy.

As it was she had no time to brood over the problems created by Feckenham's attitude and behaviour. There were messages to be sent, letters and goodbye presents to be considered, two attendants to be chosen out of her suite to witness her death and 'decently dispose' her body, and a suitable dress selected for her appearance on the scaffold. Although all these matters were subordinated to her spiritual preparations, they must not be neglected. She began with the letters.

On February 10th, while Bishop Gardiner, preaching before Queen Mary, insisted that Lady Jane as one of the 'rotten and hurtful members of the Commonweal' should be cut off,[20] she was writing a letter to her sister Katherine on the blank pages of her Greek Testament. This document – it can hardly be described as a personal communication – is almost wholly scriptural and reads like an essay. Beginning with 'I have sent you, good sister Katherine, a book which, although it be not outwardly trimmed with gold, yet inwardly it is more worth than precious stones', Lady Jane outlined the principal points of its contents and went on, 'It will teach you to live and learn you to die; it shall win you more than you should have gained by the possession of your woeful father's lands.' After a long instructive passage, the writer bids Lady Katherine, 'Rejoice, as I do, and adsist [consider] that I shall be delivered of this corruption, and put on incorruption, for I am assured

that I shall, for losing of a mortal life, find an immortal felicity.' She then adjures her sister to continue in the fear of God,
'to your comfort and His glory, to the which glory God bring
mine and you hereafter, when it shall please God to call you'.[21]

To her father, who had sent her agonized messages of re-
morse, she wrote twice, in a gentler and more human strain.
Her first reply, written in the Prayer Book which she carried
to the scaffold, is short and simple. 'The Lord comfort Your
Grace, and that in His word wherein all creatures only are to
be comforted, and though it hath pleased God to take away
two of your children, yet think not, I most humbly beseech
Your Grace, that you have lost them, but trust that we, by
losing this mortal life have won an immortal life, and I, for my
part, as I have honoured Your Grace in this life will pray for
you in another life, Your Grace's humble daughter, Jane
Duddeley [sic].'[22]

This reassurance was followed by a longer and more deeply
felt communication, beginning, 'Father, Although it hath
pleased God to hasten my death by you, by whom my life
should rather have been lengthened, yet can I so patiently take
it that I yield God more hearty thanks for shortening my woeful days than if all the world had been given into my possession[s] with life lengthened at my own will. And albeit I am
very well assured of your impatient dolours ... yet, my dear
Father, if I may without offence rejoice in my own mishaps,
herein I may account myself blessed, that, washing my hands
with the innocency of my fact [actions], my guiltless blood
may cry before the Lord ...' Lady Jane's sense of injury then
combines with her acknowledgement of justice in a passage in
which the omission of the key word is curiously significant.
'And yet, though I must needs acknowledge that being con-
strained and (as you know well enough) continually assayed,
yet in taking up on me [the crown] I seemed to consent and
therein grievously offended the Queen and her laws.' She then
reverts to her willingness to die: 'To me there is nothing that
can be more welcome than from this vale of misery to aspire
to that heavenly throne of all joy and pleasure with Christ my
Saviour.' She asks God to strengthen Suffolk in his own ordeal,

and concludes, 'The Lord ... continue to keep you, that at the last we may meet in Heaven with the Father, the Son and the Holy Ghost ... Your obedient daughter till death.'[23]

The Lieutenant of the Tower having asked her for a remembrance, she decided to give him her little velvet Prayer Book, in which she wrote, 'Forasmuch as you have desired so simple a woman to write in so worthy a book, good Master Lieutenant, therefore I shall as a friend, desire you, and as a Christian require you, to call upon God, to incline your heart to His laws, to quicken you in His way, and not to take the word of truth utterly out of your mouth. Live still to die, that by death you may purchase eternal life ... The preacher saith, There is a time to be born and a time to die, and the day of our death is better than the day of our birth. Yours, as the Lord knoweth, a true friend.'[24] The handwriting on these pages is delicate and clear; it gives the impression that Lady Jane had found pleasure in composing this particular fare----[11]

And now, there only remained her speech from the scaffold, which must be written out so that it might be published after her death. This, the testament of her political and spiritual convictions, was the most important of all; for in it she must declare both her innocence and her guilt. She had broken the law, and thus offended God; for in usurping her cousin's right she had insulted the Deity whose representative Mary was. Although it must be made clear that in one sense she had been forced into that position, she must yet revert to the moment in Sion House when she had asked God whether she should accept the crown or not – and had received no answer. In taking that silence for consent she had committed her greatest sin.

She was in the midst of this composition when a message came to her from the Queen. Guilford had asked and obtained leave to say goodbye to her; it was for her to decide when he should do so.[25]

It is possible that Lady Jane had forgotten all about the handsome and wilful young man whom his father's doting ambition had destroyed. Her reply seems to indicate that his irruption into her last hours came as a disagreebale reminder of sin, error and the fear of death.

Guilford, now in his eighteenth year, was not resigned; he cried a great deal,[26] and may have hoped to draw strength and comfort from his wife, although she had sent him no letters or messages. Her brief answer to this, the request of a dying man, was not, from his point of view, very consoling. She preferred not to meet and desired him to 'omit these moments of grief', adding, 'for we shall shortly behold each other in a better place'.[27] Then she turned again to her prayers and meditations.

Her last farewell to the world of the living was contained in three sentences, the first in Latin, the second in Greek, the third in English. They were: 'If justice is done with my body, my soul will find mercy with God. Death will give pain to my body for its sins, but the soul will be justified before God. If my faults deserve punishment, my youth at least, and my imprudence were worthy of excuse; God and posterity will show me favour.'[28]

These aphorisms, the distillation of her philosophy, were composed on the night of February 11th. At ten o'clock the next morning she and Guilford were to die – he on Tower Hill, she, as became a princess of the blood, privately, on Tower Green. She had promised to watch him go to the place of execution. When the time came she was standing in the window, dressed in the black gown she had worn at her trial.[29] She had just submitted to the final and somewhat degrading ordeal of 'examination by a body of matrons' in the event of her having become pregnant.[30]

iii

No attempt had been made to convert Guilford Dudley, and he himself did not suggest that he should see a priest. On the morning of the 12th he asked that a Protestant clergyman might accompany him to the scaffold and was told that this was not allowed.[31] Such harsh treatment distressed the Tower officials, most of whom shared Guilford's beliefs, and they decided to make it up to him by attentions of a different kind. Sir Anthony Browne, Master of the Horse, Sir John Throckmorton and 'many other gentlemen' came with the Lieutenant of the Tower to escort him to the outer bulwarks, where Sir Thomas Offeley, Sheriff of London, waited to walk with him to the scaffold; on Devil's Tower, Northampton, now reinstated as Lord High Treasurer and thus representing the Queen, stood to watch his execution.[32]

Lady Jane's sight of him was momentary; from the Gentleman-Gaoler's lodgings she could have caught no more than a glimpse of the procession surrounding the tall slight figure. She was now within half an hour, or less, of her own death; for she knew that the ceremonies on Tower Hill would be curtailed, as Guilford was not likely to be capable of a long speech. The headsman would then return to await her on Tower Green. She therefore decided to pay her tribute by waiting to watch Guilford's body brought back to St Peter-ad-Vincula.[33]

It was said afterwards that 'these two simple young souls' were separately executed in order to 'avoid commotions', and that Queen Mary's refusal to reprieve them so roused the pity and wrath of the people as permanently to destroy her popularity.[34] This view was that of the Protestant chroniclers of the next decade, some of whom declared that the Queen had instructed the authorities to force Lady Jane to see the return of her husband's headless corpse in order to torture her.[35] It was not so. Lady Jane herself had decided to stay by the window, for reasons that she did not explain.[36]

When he reached the scaffold Guilford shook hands with his companions and asked them to pray for him. He had been too much agitated to write out a speech, but so far complied with etiquette as to make a 'very small declaration' to the crowd.[37] He knelt to pray. Then, raising his clasped hands, he sobbed out 'Pray for me – pray for me!' several times.[38] His eyes were bandaged and he was led to the block. The headsman did his business with one stroke.[39]

Guilford's head was then wrapped in a cloth; that, and his body were thrown into a hand-cart and wheeled back through the main gateway, past the Beauchamp Tower and so underneath the window where Lady Jane was standing. There, says an eyewitness, 'she did see his dead carcase taken out of the cart . . . a sight to her no less than death'.[40]

She broke down, not into tears, but into sudden, agonized compassion for the poor boy she had never been able to like. She said. 'O! Guilford – Guilford!', and those near heard her murmur something about 'the bitterness of death'.[41]

By the time Guilford's head and body had been carried into the chapel the headsman and his assistant had taken up their positions on the scaffold of the Green. Lady Jane waited for the procession to form. Then she came out – 'nothing at all abashed', according to the same spectator[42] – walking between Feckenham and Sir John Bridges, her Prayer Book in her hand. Nurse Ellen and Mrs Tilney, who 'wonderfully wept', were behind her,[43] the halberdiers in front and on either side. The private audience surrounding the scaffold was a large one; everybody who had been able to get permission to see her die was there.

What chiefly struck those who have left an account of both executions was the contrast between Lady Jane's and her husband's behaviour. He had wept all the way to the scaffold; she remained serene and dry-eyed; one hand was on the arm of the Lieutenant, who was leading her; in the other she held her Prayer Book, reading in it as she walked.[44] To those who had seen her only in public she looked like a child; for without her chopines she was dwarfed by the men surrounding her. So it was that when she mounted the scaffold the block and axe were hidden from her by the towering, scarlet-clad shape of the headsman.

It was now time for her to address the spectators. With characteristic circumspection she turned to Sir John Bridges and said, 'Can I speak what is in my mind?' He replied, 'Yes, Madam,' and she came to the rail.[45] Her voice was steady and distinct as she began – 'Good people – I am come hither to die, and by a law I am condemned to the same. My offence against the Queen's Highness was only in consent to the devices of others, which now is deemed treason; but it was never of my seeking, but by counsel of those who should seem to have further understanding of things than I, which knew little of the law, and much less of the titles to the crown. But touching the procurement and desire thereof by me, or on my behalf, I do wash my hands in innocency thereof before God, and in the face of all you good Christian people this day.'

As she said this she wrung her hands, in one of which she still held her Prayer Book. Then she resumed, 'I pray you all, good Christian people, to bear me witness that I die a true Christian woman, and that I look to be saved by none other means but only by the mercy of God, in the blood of His only Son, Jesus Christ. And I confess that when I did know the word of God, I neglected the same, and loved myself and the world, and therefore this plague and punishment is justly and worthily happened unto me for my sins — and yet I thank God of His goodness that He hath given me a time and respite to repent.' The last words of her speech were a demonstration of one of the most important tenets of her faith. 'And now, good people, *while I am alive*, I pray you assist me with your prayers.'[46]

She turned to Feckenham, who was standing behind her, and said, 'Shall I say this Psalm?' It was one she had already chosen, and knew by heart — the Fifty-First. He could not answer at once. Then those nearest heard him say, 'Yea.' Lady Jane knelt, folded her hands and began 'Have mercy upon me, O God, according to Thy loving-kindness ...' all through the nineteen verses, while he, also kneeling, followed her in Latin.

When she ended they both got up and there was a moment's pause. Then Lady Jane said, 'God I beseech Him abundantly reward you for your kindness towards me.' She added with an irrepressible burst of candour, 'Although I must needs say, it was more unwelcome to me than my instant death is terrible.'[47]

Feckenham was silent. His long and intimate experience of the human spirit, his skill and sympathy, his gift for the right word — all failed him as he looked down at the small, steadfast face under the black hood. Lady Jane saw his distress. She leaned forward and kissed him.[48] For a moment they remained standing hand in hand.[49]

It was then the custom for the proceedings to be halted for some minutes in the event of a reprieve. As Lady Jane's refusal to apostasize had disposed of this contingency, she went on with her preparations. She said goodbye to Sir John Bridges and gave him her Prayer Book. Then she summoned her nurse, to whom she gave her handkerchief and gloves. As she began to untie the upper part of her gown the headsman came forward, ostensibly to help her, but in fact with the intention of taking it as part of his fee. Lady Jane said, 'Let me alone —' and he stood back. Nurse Ellen was too much agitated to be of use, and Mrs Tilney had to help her. Yet neither was able to perform the final duty – that of blindfolding their mistress – and so she was left standing with the 'fair handkerchief',[50] carefully selected three days ago, in her hand. The executioner approached her again. He knelt and said, 'Do you forgive me, Madam?' 'Most willingly,' Lady Jane replied.

The headsman got up and made way for her. Then she saw the block. It was surrounded by piles of straw. She stood looking at it. The headsman said, 'Stand upon the straw, Madam.'

Still she did not move. At last she said 'I pray you – dispatch me quickly —' and came nearer. She knew what to do. Having knelt, she must place her head in the curved aperture, and give the executioner the signal by stretching out her arms.

Until this moment she had not been afraid, because she was alone with God: almost in the next world. Now, in a silence broken only by her women's sobbing and the rustle of the straw, her neck and shoulders suddenly exposed to the cutting air, she came back. It was as if she had begun to feel that slashing stroke – and there might be more than one – already. The headsman was standing over her. She said, 'Will you take it off before I lay me down?' 'No, Madam,' said the huge masked figure.

Lady Jane tied the handkerchief over her eyes. She put out her hands, feeling for the block. She had misjudged the distance. It was not there. She cried out, 'Where is it? Where is it?' There was no reply.

She was surrounded by professionals, adepts in the arrangement and performance of executions. None of them – neither Sir John Bridges, nor the attendant officials, nor the headsman nor his assistant – came to help her. She cried out again, 'What shall I do?' Still they stood silent, appalled, unable to move. At last someone standing beyond the rail climbed up and guided her towards the block.

Now the small black shape was kneeling, its arms outstretched. The headsman raised the axe, poising it, legs apart. Lady Jane said loudly and clearly, 'Lord, into Thy hands I commend my spirit.'

Then came the crash. A round, dark object rolled beyond the block. Blood poured from it, over the scaffold – and from the obscene, meaningless fragment lying in the straw. The executioner stooped, fumbled, stood up. His voice rang out across the Green. 'So perish all the Queen's enemies! Behold the head of a traitor!'[51]

NOTES

1. Cobbett, *State Trials*, vol I, p 868.
2. Foxe, *Acts and Monuments*, vol VI, p 423.
3. Harleian MSS, 2194.
4. Jowett's translation.
5. Becon, *Early Works*, p 55.
6. *Cal SP Spanish*, vol XII, p 87.
7. Jardine, *State Trials*, vol I, p 43.
8. *Cal SP Spanish*, vol XII, p 94.
9. Ibid.
10. Strype, *Ecclesiastical Memorials*, vol III, pt 1, p 141.
11. Knowles, *The Religious Orders in England*, vol III, p 431.
12. *Original Letters*, vol I, p 303.
13. Foxe, vol VI, pp 415–16.
14. Nicolas, *Memoirs and Literary Remains of Lady Jane Grey*, p 1; Godwin, *Annals of England*, p 296.
15. Nicolas, p 1.
16. Foxe, vol VI, pp 415–16.
17. Ibid.
18. Ibid.
19. *Original Letters*, vol II, p 303.
20. *Queen Jane and Queen Mary*, ed Nichols, p 54.
21. Harleian MSS, 2342.
22. Ibid.
23. Ibid.

24. Ibid.
25. Foxe, vol VI, p 415.
26. *Queen Jane and Queen Mary*, p 54.
27. Godwin, p 296; Baker, *Chronicle*, p 96.
28. Florio, *Historia de la vita ... Giovanna Graia*, p 60.
29. Holinshed, *Chronicle*, vol IV, p 23.
30. Foxe, vol VI, p 415.
31. *Queen Jane and Queen Mary*, p 54.
32. Ibid, Fuller, vol II, p 226.
33. *Queen Jane and Queen Mary*, p 54.
34. Cobbett, vol I, p 721.
35. Florio, p 131.
36. Cobbett, vol I, p 721.
37. Holinshed, vol IV, p 22; *Queen Jane and Queen Mary*, p 55.
38. Ibid.
39. Ibid.
40. Ibid.
41. Florio, p 76.
42. *Queen Jane and Queen Mary*, p 55.
43. Ibid.
44. Ibid, p 56; Holinshed, vol IV, p 22.
45. Florio, p 131.
46. *Queen Jane and Queen Mary*, p 55; Holinshed, vol IV, p 22.
47. Godwin, p 295.
48. Pollini, *Historia Ecclesiastica*, pp 260–97.
49. De Thou, *History of His Own Time*, vol I, p 620.
50. Holinshed, vol IV, p 22.
51. Ibid; *Queen Jane and Queen Mary*, p 55.

Epilogue

SUFFOLK and Wyatt were executed in the last week of February 1554. Lord Thomas Grey followed them to the block in April; Lord John was fined and released. Some three weeks after her husband's death Frances Suffolk married her steward, Adrian Stokes, a handsome, underbred young man in his twenties; nine months later she gave birth to a daughter who died in infancy; she herself died in 1559. Katherine and Mary Grey lived to fulfil more pitiable if less dramatic destinies than Lady Jane; their stories have been told elsewhere.[1]

Of the four surviving Dudley brothers, only Robert, who was condemned to death during the Wyatt rebellion, rose to his father's greatness and power as Earl of Leicester. John Earl of Warwick, released early in 1554, died at Penshurst ten days after his return there; Ambrose inherited his title and served Queen Elizabeth till his death in 1590; Henry was killed in France in 1555. Mary as Lady Sidney and Katherine as Countess of Huntingdon enjoyed peaceful and honourable old age. When Elizabeth succeeded, Feckenham was sent to the Tower, where he died twenty years later.

Of Lady Jane's Councillors and betrayers, Arundel, who became Steward of the Household to both Mary and Elizabeth, was the only one to leave no issue; the descendants of Pembroke, Huntingdon, Winchester, Northampton and Cecil continued the family traditions of profitable service to the State, respectably and with integrity. Judge Morgan became very ill some six months after he passed sentence on Jane and Guilford. Falling into delirium, he was perpetually haunted by a black-clad shape which rose to stare at him from the foot of his bed. In his agony he cried out, 'Take the Lady Jane from me! Take away Lady Jane!' – and died raving.[2]

That discordant echo was soon drowned by the mellifluous elegies of the Protestant historians. In cooing adulation, with reverential lyricism, they continued to celebrate – and to multiply – the virtues of their favourite heroine. Early in the eighteenth century, Bradgate became a picturesque ruin, as the result of a fire; and then her apotheosis was complete. In strophe and antistrophe the strain of praise soared over the prospect of her birthplace, chiming and blending in endless harmonies of graceful tribute and agreeable melancholy. 'The innocency of childhood, the beauty of youth, the birth of a princess, the learning of a clerk ... contented to sit while others endeavoured to crown her ... This worthy lady ... made misery itself amiable ... Comparable to the Mother of the Gracchi ...'[3] Nor was Guilford, the poor spoilt boy crying for his mother, neglected by the age of sensibility. He became a 'goodly and godly gentleman', whose unselfish love for his wife was eventually epitomized in an anonymous poem entitled 'A Letter from Lady Jane Grey to Lord Guilford Dudley'. Here, in smooth rhyming couplets, Jane reminds Guilford of their pure affections and bids him farewell with elegant restraint. And so that bitter February morning – the huge masked headsman – the scaffold soaked in blood – the kneeling figure the voice crying 'Where is it? What shall I do?' were forgotten.

Perhaps it is as well. Otherwise, Bradgate Park, with its large-eyed, lightly springing deer, its rocks and ferns and the dark glitter of its stream, might not be such a pleasant place; although some of the oaks – pollarded, according to tradition, when the tenants heard that Lady Jane had been beheaded – do look rather odd, even a little sinister. The tower where, according to the same convenient belief, she read the *Phaedo* and talked with Ascham, is not much more decayed than the rest; traces of Suffolk's brickworks and slate-quarries barely mar the romantic gloom of the scene.

But for those who like their history rather less highly varnished, there remains that small, square book in the Manuscript Room of the British Museum; and the prayer, faint but still just legible, in the neat 'Roman' hand of the early sixteenth century – 'O Father, deliver us from Thy everlasting wrath and the punishments of hell. Deliver us from Thy strait judgement and at the last day of doom. Deliver us from sudden death ...'

NOTES

1. Chapman, *Two Tudor Portraits*; Davcy, *The Sisters of Lady Jane Grey*; Strickland, *Lives of the Tudor and Stuart Princesses.*

2. Holinshed, *Chronicle,* vol IV, p 23.

3. Nichols, *Leicestershire,* vol. III, pp 666–7.

Bibliography

Acts of the Privy Council (vols I, IV)

Allen J., *A History of Political Thought in the Sixteenth Century*

Antiquarian Repertory, ed F. Grose and T. Astle (vol IV)

Archaeologia (vol V)

Ascham, R., *Toxophilus*
            The Schoolmaster

Aylmer, J., *Harbour for Faithful Subjects*

Baker, R., *Chronicle*

Baschet, A., *La Diplomatie Vénitienne*

Bacon, T., *Early Works*

Besant, W., *London in the Tudor Age*

Bindoff, S., *Tudor England*

Burnet G., *History of the Reformation of the Church of England*

Calendar of State Papers: Domestic
                        Spanish
                        Venetian

Carte, T., *History of England*

Chapman, H., *The Last Tudor King*
              Two Tudor Portraits

Cobbett, W., *State Trials* (vol I)

Collins, A., *Letters and Memorials of State*

Davey, R., *Lady Jane Grey and Her Times*
            The Sisters of Lady Jane Grey

Einstein, L., *Tudor Ideals*

Ellis, H., *Original Letters Illustrative of English History*
          III)

Elton, G. R., *England under the Tudors*

Elyot, T., *The Governor*

Florio, M., *Historia de la vita ... Giovanna Graia*

Foxe, J., *Acts and Monuments* (vols VI, VIII)

Froude, J., *History of England* (vol V)

Fuller, T., *The Worthies of England*
       Holy State

Furnivall, F., *Early English Meals and Manners*

Godwin, F., *Annals of England*

Grafton, R., *Chronicle*

Granvelle, Cardinal, *Papiers d'Etat* (vol IV)

Graziani, A., *Life of Cardinal Commendone*

Griffet, Père, *Nouveaux Eclaircissements sur l'Histoire de Marie Reine d'Angleterre*

Guaras, A. de., *The Accession of Queen Mary*

Harbison E., *Rival Ambassadors at the Court of Queen Mary*

Harington, J., *Nugae Antiquae*

Harleian MSS, 2342, 2194

Harrison, W., *Description of England*

Haynes, S., ed., *Burleigh State Papers*

Hayward, J., *Life of Edward VI*

Heylyn, P., *History of the Reformation*

Holinshed, R., *Chronicle*

Howard, G., *Life of Lady Jane Grey*

Jardine, A., *State Trials* (vol I)

Jones, W., *Crowns and Coronations*

Knowles, D., *The Religious Orders in England* (vol III)

Lansdowne MSS, 1236

Laver, J., *Early Tudor Costume*

Lodge, E., *Portraits of Illustrious Personages in Great Britain* (vol II)

Lords' *Journals*

Losely MSS

Machyn, H., *Diary*

Mackic, J., *The Earlier Tudors 1485–1558*

Madden, F., *Expenses of Princess Mary*

Middleton MSS

Morris, G. C., *The Tudors*
       Political Thoughts in England: Tyndale to Hooker

Nichols, J., *History of Leicestershire* (vols III, IV)
Nichols, J. G., ed., *Life of Lord Arundel*
                Greyfriars Chronicle
                Literary Remains of Edward VI
                Narratives of the Reformation
                Queen Jane and Queen Mary
Nicolas, N. H., *Memoirs and Literary Remains of Lady Jane Grey*
Northumberland MSS
Nugent, E., *The Thought and Culture of the English Renaissance*
Nugent-Bell, H., *The Huntingdon Peerage*
Paget, G., *Leicestershire*
Parker Society, *Original Letters*
Parr, K., *Lamentations of a Sinner*
Plato, *The Phaedo* (B. Jowett's translation)
Pollard, A., *England under Protector Somerset*
              Political History of England
Pollini, G., *Historia Ecclesiastica*
Prescott, H., *Mary Tudor*
Rapin de Thoyras, P. de, *History of England* (vol. III)
Raumer, F. von, *History of the Sixteenth and Seventeenth Centuries*
              Illustrations to British History
Raviglio, Rosso, G., *Historia delle cose occorse nel regno d'Inghilterra*
Read, C., *Mr Secretary Cecil and Queen Elizabeth*
Salzmann, L., *England in Tudor Times*
Sidney, P., *Jane the Quene*
Speed, J., *History of Great Britain*
Stow, J., *Annals of England*
Strickland, A., *Lives of the Tudor and Stuart Princesses*
              Lives of the Queens of England (vol II)
Strype, J., *Annals of the Reformation*
              Ecclesiastical Memorials
              Lives of Cranmer, Parker, Aylmer and Cheke
Thou, J. de, *History of His Own Time* (vol I)

Throckmorton, N., *The Legend of Sir Nicholas Throckmorton*, ed Nichols

Turner, S., *History of England*

Tytler, P., *England under the Reigns of Edward VI and Mary*

Vertot, R., *Ambassades de MM de Noailles*

Watson, F., *Vives and the Renaissance Education of Women*

Wriothesley, C., *Journal*

History and Biography